Infrastructure for Knowledge Management

Randy J. Frid, Ph.D., MCSE, MCT

e-mail: dr.frid@frid.com
website: www.frid.com

Writers Club Press
San Jose • New York • Lincoln • Shanghai

Dedication

This book is dedicated to Betty and Jonas Frid, my parents. Long before Knowledge Management was ever a buzzword they were masters in the art of knowledge transfer. It was only as I grew older and had to teach my own children, that I've learned to truly appreciate their incredible talent to mentor, and for creating a perfect environment for the cultivation of knowledge and imagination.

Table of Contents

COMMON VOCABULARY

Throughout this book we will frequently use terminology not common to our daily workplace, so I'll use Merriam-Webster to begin establishing a common vocabulary that we can live with:

tac·it

1 : expressed or carried on without words or speech
2 a : implied or indicated but not actually expressed <*tacit* consent>
  b (1) : arising without express contract or agreement
    (2) : arising by operation of law <*tacit* mortgage>

ex·plic·it

1 a : fully revealed or expressed without vagueness, implication, or
    ambiguity : leaving no question as to meaning or intent
    <*explicit* instructions>
  b : open in the depiction of nudity or sexuality
    <*explicit* books and films>
2 : fully developed or formulated <an *explicit* plan>
    <an *explicit* notion of our objective>
3 : unambiguous in expression
    <was very *explicit* on how we are to behave>

in·ter·po·late

1 a : to alter or corrupt (as a text) by inserting new or foreign matter
  b : to insert (words) into a text or into a conversation
2 : to insert between other things or parts : **INTERCALATE**
3 : to estimate values of (a function) between two known values
    intransitive senses : to make insertions (as of estimated values)

Meta

Etymology: New Latin & Medieval Latin, from Latin or Greek; Latin, from Greek, among, with, after, from *meta* among, with, after; akin to Old English *mid, mith* with, Old High German *mit*
1 a : occurring later than or in succession to : after <*met*estrus>
  b : situated behind or beyond <*met*encephalon> <*meta*carpus>
  c : later or more highly organized or specialized form of <*meta*xylem>

heu·ris·tic

: involving or serving as an aid to learning, discovery, or problem-solving by experimental and especially trial-and-error methods <*heuristic* techniques> <a *heuristic* assumption>; *also* : of or relating to exploratory problem-solving techniques that utilize self-educating techniques (as the evaluation of feedback) to improve performance <a *heuristic* computer program>

INTRODUCTION

Albert Einstein once stated; **"Imagination is more important than knowledge"**. He was right.

You can absorb all the knowledge your mind can hold but if you don't have the imagination to apply it to something innovative, you add no value, either to the knowledge itself or to your organization, who's very survival depends on innovation.

After writing this book, I looked back and thought, "Knowledge Management is complicated." Over the years I've been picking up parts of the jigsaw puzzle and testing them here and there. But it wasn't until I forced myself to start putting things down on paper that the shear quantity of pieces became apparent. What also become quickly apparent were the missing pieces. Thus began my research effort to find the missing sacred knowledge.

On the road to adventure I found something a little shocking. I had been developing *my* pieces of the jigsaw puzzle by myself over the years and was quite comfortable in their validity (you can always rationalize your own ideas). When I began looking into other peoples writings and opinions on knowledge and knowledge management I found the ideas numerous and often differing vastly in even their fundamental concepts. Some ideas were shallow, not delving deep enough under the covers, and some ideas were way too deep, requiring the readers to take enormous leaps of faith in the rationale. Others were far too technical, written by computer geeks, demonstrating how a simple 10 billion dollar investment in technology and the hiring of

10,000 programmers would define how knowledge flowed through your enterprise. They didn't tell you what you would do with this knowledge but at least there were lots of "blinky lights".

It took a lot of digging to finally uncover some concepts I personally considered worth at least the paper they were written on. Eventually I was able to complete the jigsaw puzzle (or at least enough of it to understand what the picture was going to look like at the end).

That's when I realized I had better include in this section, a summary of knowledge management, so there is a frame of reference before we begin digging deeper into the different areas throughout the book.

Let's start off by giving knowledge management a definition:

"Knowledge Management serves two masters. First, knowledge management is required to extract knowledge from our brains and transfer it to other systems or people. Second, knowledge management is required to extract information from systems and present it to our brain."

Next, I'll tell you that knowledge management works by moving the two fundamental types of knowledge from imagination to reality, then back again:

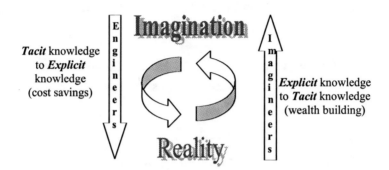

You'll also notice that I used Disney's term "Imagineers" for the knowledge managers that are required to move the Explicit knowledge back to Tacit knowledge. This is because there are significant differences between the two types of knowledge managers (Engineers and Imagineers) and I just liked Disney's terminology. Besides, they have a long and proven record for turning Imagination into Reality and vise versa.

Knowledge Imagineer Focus	Knowledge Engineer Focus
Customers Perceived Value	Internal Process Development
Non-Customers Perceived Value	Internal Process Automation
Market Changes	End-to-End Viability Analysis
Demographics	Quality Assurance
Political Environment Issues	Results Measurement
Economic Environment Issues	Process Re-Engineering
Current and Future Competition	Project Management Framework
New Technologies Outside Industry	Management Controls
Training Programs	IT Technologies
Communications	Standards and Policies
Knowledge Mapping	Knowledge Programs

This is the scope of the Knowledge Manager and the role in which knowledge management plays in an enterprise. The bottom line is that we push knowledge back and forth between Imagination and Reality to achieve different objectives.

We push knowledge from Tacit to Explicit to achieve results, and we push knowledge from Explicit to Tacit to stimulate the imagination to create innovation.

In either regard, knowledge management does *not* teach people how to use their imagination. Organizations are going to have to rely on their Human Resource departments to find and hire those people that are actually capable of using their imagination to turn knowledge into innovation. Knowledge Management also does not teach personal motivation to those without it. After all, having a wealth of knowledge and a powerful imagination is still useless if one is not motivated to do something about it. You can lead a horse to water...

Mother Nature pre-programmed all life to endlessly seek out the optimum genetic code for a specific environment. As the environment changes, so do the criteria that life forms look for and consider the optimum genetic code *at that time*. Companies and Organizations are no different. They need to *endlessly* seek the optimum configuration, customers, suppliers, products and services that best suit the environment of the moment.

Knowledge management provides assistance in the corporate genetic search adventure and the rest of this book will hopefully bring you closer to obtaining the goal of better assessing your environment and determining which tools can assist in your knowledge management endeavors.

CHAPTER 1—
Defining Knowledge Management

Knowledge Management means many things to many people. The term Knowledge Management has been represented from specific products to complete systems but seems to be referenced mostly from the technological perspective. It still amazes me how many organizations I speak to, start with the question "What product should we choose?" Others I also run up against all the time state, "We're doing knowledge management. We have Lotus Notes".

Let's start by stating what knowledge management is NOT. That may put a clear light on the direction of this chapter.

Knowledge management is **NOT** the following:

- Desktop Productivity Software
- Email and PIM Software
- Groupware or Collaborative Software
- Data Warehousing & Mining Software
- ERP Software
- Business Process Automation Software
- E-Commerce Software
- Search Software

Technology is currently limited in what aspects of knowledge management it can participate in, at this time. We can utilize technology to help us capture and deliver certain types of information or to provide us a conduit between people with knowledge. Technology cannot currently handle the highest-level knowledge functions that the human mind performs. This high-level functioning is called *imagination* from which springs *innovation*. Computers are nowhere near the capacity of the human mind for this type of processing. Only with the inclusion of a currently non-existing intelligence could they come close. The shear magnitude of variables and interrelationships the human mind must juggle to extract a single meaningful thought cannot be programmed by using traditional logic.

As a good example, there was a financial organization that managed mutual funds that had a senior analyst that was nearing retirement. The track record of this man to accurately assess the quality of companies to include in the portfolio was very impressive. The financial company didn't want to lose this skill and hired a computer scientist to work with this man over the next two years before retirement to develop a program that would capture the analyst's process of assessment.

Day after day the two men worked to develop the software system and the scientist drilled down on every single nuance and variable the analyst could articulate. After a year and a half the financial company reviewed the project for the final time and decided to scrap the entire project. The software that had been developed up to that point was producing completely inaccurate results and no one could figure out what it would take to fix the problems.

The interesting result of the project was that, although the computer solution turned out completely useless, the computer scientist performing the research was now a very skilled financial analyst.

Let's understand up front that technology does not create knowledge, only the human mind can accomplish this today, but technology can and does play a part in today's knowledge *management* efforts.

Knowing that technology does play a part in knowledge management, we still need to recognize that the heart of knowledge management lies not in technology but in the building of processes to support a Learning, Remembering and Mentoring based enterprise.

In building a Learning based enterprise we need to discern how we create knowledge so we can begin understanding how we can manage it. Once we have learnt then we need to "Remember", which means we need to develop processes, methodologies and systems that enable us to store and retrieve the knowledge we've created. Finally we need to "Mentor" others in our knowledge and build infrastructure to help us disseminate the knowledge to reduce redundancy, provide common intake and feed the innovation pipeline.

The Meaning of "Knowledge"

Let's start by clarifying the meaning of knowledge. The idea of Knowledge has been debated for centuries. Plato described it in earliest terms in "The Republic" as being a State of Mind. I believe, at this point in time, that knowledge would be better described as being a State of Certification.

Knowledge can be categorized in two ways:

   1. **Tacit** (requires us to interpret information and apply judgment)
   2. **Explicit** (enough certification to remove doubt and the need to interpret)

Tacit knowledge is largely opinion based and deemed conjectural because of partial or limited evidence and unqualified interpolative data. There is always insufficient supporting evidence to remove doubt in Tacit knowledge.

Explicit knowledge is fact and is qualified with adequate supporting evidence and context that demonstrates enough reconciliation to remove doubt.

All Knowledge must also be weighed in its current context. Consider that Explicit knowledge may provide enough evidence to remove doubt, but the evidence may only be supportive under specific circumstances. Changing the context may change a fact to an opinion or an opinion into supposition. As an example, consider the color yellow. A yellow Volkswagen beetle would be deemed yellow if you maintained a similar velocity with the car. If you were to accelerate the car near the speed of light then you would deem the car to be green if it was traveling towards you, as the light would shift towards the blue spectrum. If the car were accelerating away from you, you would say the car was orange in color, as the light would be shifting towards the red spectrum. We can conclude that knowledge is only Explicit in its given context. Context is therefore critical to the certification of Explicit knowledge.

Management of Explicit knowledge offers the most immediate impact for commercial organizations. Explicit knowledge is usually internal to an organization and is easily collected and assimilated into storage and delivery systems. Explicit knowledge is usually referred too as process or contextual information. Our objective with Explicit knowledge is to capture process or contextual information into technology to provide rapid and easy access to known facts.

"Collecting" may not be the right term to describe our objectives for Tacit knowledge. In essence our objective for Tacit knowledge would more or less be the creation of a "knowledge map" that can point us quickly and efficiently to the repository of relevant Tacit knowledge, which resides only in the minds of humans. We'll discuss this in greater detail later on in Chapter 6—HELP.

Plato also described knowledge in mathematical terms in order to demonstrate that knowledge is not based solely on the consensus of our five senses. Using a "point" as an example, a point is purely theoretical, as we cannot demonstrate a point with no dimensions and no start or finish. Since this concept is held in the human mind we refer to this knowledge as Tacit instead of Explicit.

Does Explicit knowledge really just mean we have enough perceived evidence to convince someone else to remove doubt? If this is the case then anyone that can remove someone else's doubt about something in essence has created a fact in that specific context, but not necessarily the truth. Determination of the quality of knowledge is also a factor. In the absence of quality knowledge people will typically lean towards immediate or fast knowledge as opposed to performing the necessary research to find the best knowledge. This makes the location and ease of retrieval of quality knowledge significant in a knowledge management system (KMS).

Tacit knowledge is much more difficult to collect and assimilate as it typically requires an extrapolation of existing information and the input of interpolative information. Context becomes more ambiguous with Tacit knowledge and therefore also introduces additional doubt. Tacit knowledge is stored in the minds of humans and therefore humans themselves have to become extensions of the KMS as they are the only resource for Tacit knowledge.

It's essential that the senior officers and the knowledge management team have a shared vision that incorporates the definition of Knowledge and the nature of the knowledge management mission.

With the definition and mission statement providing the frame of reference then the delivery issues inherent to knowledge management do not revolve around the meaning of knowledge as much as what systems we need or desire to build to support knowledge in it's different states and different contexts. We also need to assess the value of each type of knowledge in relation to the cost of managing it.

Perceived Gains

Building support systems for Explicit knowledge one can deliver performance-based gains that can be easily perceived and measured. Capturing rigid processes and context-based information into a computer system allows us more time to focus on analysis and validation of this Explicit knowledge and therefore provides a vehicle for testing existing knowledge and reducing time spent on "reinventing the wheel".

Building infrastructure in a corporation to support Tacit knowledge provides us gains in knowledge transfer but requires the cooperation of those individuals that will be contributing to the knowledgebase. Their cooperation is essential because Tacit knowledge requires that one or more individuals assimilate explicit information, insert interpolative information, use or create context, then finally draw conclusions that can't be fully certified. Ease of access to the right human resource at the right time is mission critical to a successful KMS focused on Tacit knowledge. Still, reaching the right person doesn't guarantee that they will participate. An entire cultural strategy must be developed to support Tacit knowledge management, which we discuss in detail in the Chapter 6.

We defined Explicit knowledge management as offering performance gains and define Tacit knowledge management as offering Innovation gains.

So the knowledge management team should first decide:

> Are you looking for performance gains?
> Are you looking for gains in innovation?
> Are you looking for both?

Then build systems, processes, methodologies and policies to implement the required solutions.

The Impact of Knowledge Management

Other than increased employee performance and innovation, what is another advantage of undertaking a Knowledge Management campaign?

The answer is *Change Creation*.

Let's ask ourselves, what is the one common denominator that all individuals interact with on a daily basis throughout an enterprise? The answer is knowledge. We require knowledge at every level of an organization to execute tasks and to grow as people.

In 1927 there was an experiment carried out at the Western Electric Company in Illinois by Elton Mayo. The experiment was called the Hawthorne experiment. Mayo hoped to discover optimum levels of plant illumination and proper timing of rest periods by experimenting with selected groups of workers. He discovered that it did not matter how the workers' environment was altered; merely being chosen for an experiment improved their productivity (the Hawthorne effect).

Mayo saw that the significant variable was not physiological but psychological. A series of experiments was performed, involving the assembly of telephone relays; test and control groups were subjected to changes in wages, rest periods, workweeks, temperature, humidity, and other factors. Output continued to increase no matter how physical conditions were varied; indeed, even when conditions were returned to what they had been before, productivity remained 25 percent above its original value. Mayo concluded that the reason for this lay in the attitudes of the workers toward their jobs and toward the company. Merely by asking their cooperation in the test, the investigators had stimulated a new attitude among the employees, who now felt themselves part of an important group whose help and advice were being sought by the company.

For this reason alone we can conclude that the sponsorship of knowledge management systems will involve everyone throughout the enterprise and will effect change. This change is psychological and will help to create a new attitude in the workplace. It's this change in attitude that will create an increase in productivity. Therefore we should strive to engage a long-term knowledge management campaign that reaches everyone in an organization and requires their input and certification of the knowledge data. The employees will react in a positive manor with a resultant increase in productivity.

So long as we provide positive change in any aspect of a workers daily life we should expect an increase in productivity. Knowledge management lends itself well to creating positive change, enterprise-wide.

If an organization is looking for primary gains in Performance then it needs to target the development of methodology, processes and systems to capture, present and analyze Explicit data.

If an organization is looking for primary gains in Innovation then it needs to target the development of methodology, processes and systems to capture, present and analyze Tacit data.

What is a Knowledge Worker

How can we manage to "Not Manage"?

We have to either define or redefine our ideals about knowledge, but we also have to redefine our concept of management.

Let's start off with the management of knowledge workers. The bottom line is, you don't. This is why knowledge management is fast becoming so predominant a conversation topic on the tongues of CEO's of knowledge-based companies. When it comes to managing knowledge workers the best that we can hope to accomplish is to work with them to help develop their roles and responsibilities, manage their performance, manage the assignment of, and measure the quality of deliverables and provide mechanisms to manage the facilitation of innovation.

Our primary deliverable from knowledge workers is quality. If or when we achieve the level of quality output we require, only then can we begin to measure the quantity of output. Of course this means you need to be able to define what quality means to you, as it will mean something different to everyone. I have found that measuring quality is usually a judgmental process as opposed to an analytical process. I have also found that putting a knowledge worker at the judgmental mercy of his or her piers is the most effective way of managing quality control. After all, knowledge workers are supposed to know more about their respective fields than their managers. This means that management will forever have difficulty assessing both performance and quality. Using piers as the control mechanism provides a reasonable level of certainty in measurement.

Pier group teams can be very powerful in the control of knowledge workers. By making pier-group teams accountable for specific deliverables and rewarding them as a team, this will usually provide rapid feedback if any one particular knowledge worker is inadequate. A team of knowledge workers will often carry the burden of an inadequate team member for a short period of time but the inevitable conclusion is that the team will get tired of an individual not pulling their weight and take internal team corrective action. If internal team actions fail then the team will almost always request that management remove the defective knowledge worker. This makes management's job of quality and performance testing much easier. Management can then focus on their primary mandate, which is: Enterprise Results and Performance. We speak in detail on team building in Chapter 6.

Words of warning though, don't send a knowledge worker into a team without carefully defining their roles and responsibilities or you are setting them and yourself up for failure. You also have to let the knowledge worker participate in the development of those roles and responsibilities as it defines the nature of their specialty, and who is better to decide on the nature of their roles and responsibilities other than knowledge workers themselves. Their participation will also provide valuable feedback to better streamline their job, remove time-wasting obstacles and develop more efficient ways of achieving their deliverables. In other words they will apply classic business process re-engineering techniques to their own job function.

Knowledge Worker vs. Unskilled Labor

We no longer get to exercise the control and domination that management concepts have held so near and dear for so long over labor workers. Why not? Because there are fewer and fewer people involved in the manual labor process component of delivering a product or service. Therefore, those "control management" practices diminish in direct proportion to the diminishing manual laborers. Manual laborers are being supplanted by modern day "knowledge workers".
Knowledge workers don't lend themselves well to "control manage-

ment" practices. So you may wonder where those unskilled laborers are disappearing too? Laborers aren't actually disappearing; they are being converted into knowledge workers.

Some of the major industries of growth include medicine, education, technology, government and financial services. These growth industries have one distinct quality in common with each other; they require knowledge workers, not unskilled labor. That's one reason countries with large populations of unskilled labor such as China, Indonesia, Korea, etc. are having so much financial difficulty, and their difficulties will continue to escalate. The demand for unskilled labor is decreasing while the demand for knowledge workers is increasing and will continue to increase. So the countries with a large population of unskilled labor are gaining an ever-increasing share of an ever-diminishing market. This is a clear sign of trouble.

The conversion of unskilled labor to knowledge worker has been most predominant in North America and Europe. Developing countries are struggling in this conversion primarily because they don't have the educational infrastructure that the United States and Canada has. Even Europe for that matter doesn't have the educational capacity of the US and Canada as their system of apprenticeship education is focused on the young and doesn't target the adult education markets. The US and Canada's post secondary educational infrastructure will provide them a definitive advantage over the next twenty years as the working population increases in age, and the inevitable lack of younger workers will require the re-education and retention of older workers.

The inevitable lack of younger workers is caused by the decreasing birthrate in developed countries. In order to sustain the population of a given country you must sustain a birth rate of 2.1 births per woman (excluding children and seniors). Europe is running about 1.5 with some European countries running below 1.0, Japan runs close to 1.3 and North America is now just under 2.0. Each of the developed country's birth rates is still on the decrease. This means if everyone started having baby's in order to catch up, it would still be about 20 years before these babies would enter the work force and probably another five years still after that before they would be of any impact. But everybody is *not* having babies so it is guaranteed that we will be faced with a diminishing younger work force and will have no choice but to attempt to retain and retrain our older work force. The US and Canada have sufficient infrastructure to handle this adult retraining effort but other developed countries do not. This will also give the US and Canada a global advantage over the next 20-25 years at least.

Organizational Structure

Before we can look at the individual knowledge worker we need to look at organizational structure in general. In Chapter 6 we talk about Culture in greater detail and focus on the concept of teams. I talk a lot about teams and team building. Teams, teams and more teams. This is definitely the org-chart flavor of the day so it seems. Does this mean that all management just needs to focus on teams? Absolutely not! Teams are not the Utopian organizational structure that researchers have so long sought after in organizational management. Teams are just one method of management. Different styles of organizational structure are best suited to whatever specific tasks people are required to perform. For example, if I was running a factory trying to squeeze as many widgets off the line as humanly possible for the lowest cost, than the procedural management in a classic control hierarchy may work best given the time, environment, economics and various other context specific variables. The same manufacturing requirements, run in a different context may require a different organizational structure.

What I'm saying is that when you need to create an organizational structure environment to support "knowledge workers", they seem most conducive to participation in team environments.

Individual Characteristics of a Knowledge Worker

Let's step back in time to the time when you and I, and the ape shared a common ancestor. Anthropologists classify us in the category of "Hunter-Gatherers". Humans and apes have the biological and social infrastructure that creates for us a loose association and community. We get together when the need arises and disband when we have no further requirement to collaborate. This goes for socializing as well as productive work. Knowledge workers are Hunter-Gatherers and will typically bind their loyalties to one person, mission or belief until they either lose faith or it no longer suits their needs. Then they move on to something more promising, based on the context of the moment. Knowledge workers are not typically motivated by money, except for the fact that they demand to get paid very well for what they know. Adding a lot more cash to the offer makes them smile more but doesn't increase their enthusiasm to the project all that much. On the other hand, if they think you are not paying enough the effects are quick and dramatic. The scale doesn't work linearly in each direction unfortunately. Knowledge workers are almost totally consumed by challenge and pier respect. They are ships of knowledge adrift on a sea of buyers, and periodically dock on someone's island long enough to trade knowledge for money, respect and most importantly, adventure.

So there it is in a nutshell. You don't manage knowledge workers, you provide them with awesome challenges and opportunities, spend your time broadcasting to the rest of the known universe how great they are so they become more marketable for the next project, wherever that may be, and pay them handsomely for the fruits they bear, not on the amount of hours they work. You NEVER ask the question "What do

WE want?". They honestly don't care what you want. You need to be asking, "What do they want?" and build the environment to attract and keep them there as long as you can. You're at their mercy. But then again, what do you care unless you're a control freak. You can't control knowledge workers, but you can control the environment and turn them loose in it to produce results. That's what you really want after all, is the end result, not the control. Why do you care how the bridge got built so long as it is exactly what the customer wants, it's the best bridge in the world, at the best price, delivered on time, and hopefully documented and reproducible after the knowledge workers have gone on to bigger and better challenges.

The fact is that knowledge workers have the upper hand today and will continue to do so for the foreseeable future. They don't need you and they don't need your company because they carry their own products in their head. You are the buyer, not them. Knowledge workers will never be employees in the classical sense, as they don't feel their survival depends on the survival of your company or on anyone that works there.

Knowledge workers are assets, not liabilities. In current cost accounting systems, all employees are deemed liabilities, as they are a cost of sales or overhead. Accounting practices list buildings and equipment as assets though. But you have to ask yourself, what exactly does a building produce that adds value to the product or service for a customer. A building is an asset yet the salesman who sold the product and brought in the profits is a liability. As you can see, traditional accounting will need to change or at least offer multi-perspective views of the organization so we see the picture from a wealth creating perspective instead of a minimalist perspective.

Knowledge workers want and need to know they are assets. Management must see them as assets. Accounting systems must see them as assets. We list our assets and liabilities in traditional accounting systems so we can assess the value of a company in the event it is to be liquidated. That seems pretty stupid to me. We don't build companies with a business plan that states our sole intention is to liquidate this company. Who would ever invest in that? We build business plans that demonstrate systems for achieving wealth. The primary way to accomplish this in the foreseeable future is through the effective application and management of knowledge workers. Therefore knowledge workers become the largest asset in the company. So our objective for today and tomorrow's management is to cultivate and capitalize on both knowledge workers and knowledge management infrastructure.

There is one unique aspect of knowledge workers that I have personally noticed over the years; Knowledge workers will very carefully measure senior management. The person who holds the reigns in an organization must be clearly in command (which is demonstrated by the respect shown by others within the company). All senior management must be able to clearly articulate the vision and mission of the company as well as they must be willing to work side-by-side with the knowledge workers to prove that management actually provides value to the company through example. No matter how excellent a project looks both from an adventure perspective as well as a respect/monetary perspective, knowledge workers absolutely hate breaking their backs in any effort while senior management just sits in their big offices on the top floor, has no idea what these knowledge workers are talking about, yet scoop the big bucks because they've got the titles.

Knowledge workers have absolutely no respect for title toting management that spend more time concerned about the current price of their stock then rolling their sleeves up and getting into the business at hand. Remember that knowledge workers don't really care about the company, they want respect and adventure and are deliverable driven in their very nature, and senior management had better get downstairs and pat them on the back, talk shop and go for a beer or senior management will not earn the necessary respect required to govern these knowledge workers. Most knowledge worker turnover can and will be attributed to this singularly important problem of senior management visibility, accountability and respect.

A note to all CEO's.

If you really want to cultivate knowledge management, team building, collaboration and knowledge-based management practices to attract and sustain innovative knowledge workers, you **MUST** train your management team to relinquish the procedural control of days gone buy. And everything starts with at the top.

I am fond of my following quote: *"If I go into an organization and find the CEO is 95% efficient and the staff is 20% efficient, then I will spend the rest of my time working to make the CEO 100% efficient."*

The CEO must apply team practices to even the topmost management staff. They are, after all, your most valuable knowledge workers. They need to hold each other accountable and test each other's knowledge constantly. As the CEO you need to stimulate creative conflict amongst the team to eliminate complacency and you need to motivate them to transfer their knowledge to their downstream teams.

The company only wants results, and knowledge workers want to see their leaders lead by example and be in their face on a regular basis. The senior management must be engaged daily and able to demonstrate value-added gray matter. The bottom line is that knowledge workers want to know if the CEO and management staff are worth investing their valuable time and knowledge in.

A note to all Managers:

All managers must come to the very quick understanding that the same brainpower that makes someone a knowledge worker instead of a manual laborer is the same brainpower that is constantly assessing the cost-benefit ratio of the situation they are in. Setup the wrong environment and the benefit diminishes rapidly. Result; knowledge workers walk. Show me a company with management staff that is more concerned with control, the share prices and the accounting and I'll show you a company struggling with the pains of attracting and retaining knowledge workers.

A lot of companies can coast for a while based on the fruits of earlier successes. Unfortunately, the world of global economics today makes the decay cycle of those successes shorter and shorter. The problems with inadequate senior management knowledge of knowledge management (say that ten times) usually shows up when organizations need to inspire additional innovation to sustain profitability and market share and can't cultivate the mandatory innovative environment for their knowledge worker staff, which includes the senior executive staff as well.

Types Of Knowledge We Should Cultivate

In this section I want to discuss some of the internal and external information that you'll likely want your knowledge management system to collect and present. In no means is this list of questions a complete guide to all the information you can or may want to assimilate into your organization, nor does it provide significant rationale behind the type of suggested information. Those topics would be a book unto

themselves and we are focused in this book on providing the infrastructure to support knowledge management. At least it's a starting point.

Internal Information

When I talk internal information I typically mean the Tacit and Explicit
information that drives our internal systems, such as our operational
processes, accounting and administrative functions. These are all part of
any companies scientific management strategy which makes this information easier to obtain in most instances than external information.

The following list of questions formulates information that can be collected as part of the knowledge management system. Some questions
may only be answered by the application of sophisticated programs.
Others may be resolved through consolidation or discovery.

How well have our results matched our expectations?

The only thing the company as an entity cares about is results
and performance. When it comes to results we need to establish
our projections and test them back against actuals. This tells us
whether or not our planning and business strategies are viable.

What should we abandon?

If you don't have a program internally to visit every service
and product you offer, and test to see if they are part of a growing, mature or declining market, then you should implement
one right away. If any product or service is in the declining
market or life cycle it *must* be systematically abandoned. You
will consume too much capitol and resources chasing a dying
product or service instead of investing in growth opportunities.

Are our current processes documented?

This is a quick kill. If you haven't documented your operational processes yet then this can provide you some quick knowledge management cost savings. Have your processes mapped and stored in the knowledge base for easy reference by everyone. Then take the time to analyze the processes and figure out if there is a better way of doing things. This is basic scientific management, simple but incredibly effective.

Here is a sample workflow process map:

Tier 1 Incident Handling Workflow

Do we clearly identify our successes and capitalize on them?

Do you have a program to identify and capitalize on your successes, no matter how large or small? If you don't, you're having serious management difficulties. Change is the one constant and we must adapt. The best example of a change management program is Mother Nature. She is constantly adapting life on this planet to enable it to survive the current environment. Nature capitalizes on the best genetic qualities of the generation before and is constantly testing (piloting) new genetic code looking for better and better solutions for survival. Your company should be no different. Your program should include regularly scheduled events that analyze every single thing you did that is deemed a success. Now, the success may have come from your excellent planning or it may have been created by unforeseen factors. Either way it's telling you something. If you planned for it, congratulations, now repeat it. If your successes caught you unawares then its time to go back to your strategy and tweak it (and then repeat it).

What opportunities should we chase?

If an opportunity presents itself, how well does it align to your business strategy? I mean, an opportunity can look really good, so good you just can't resist. The problem is you manufacture snow blowers and this is an opportunity for investment into the company that writes snow blower software. What do you know about running a software development company? Opportunities are opportunities only if they align with your strategy. Otherwise you will fragment your resources and capital. Usually these ventures, outside the realm of your strategy, cost enormous amounts of time, energy and money and offer the original company very little. Don't get me wrong, it may be very exciting for the CEO but is usually of little economic value to the enterprise.

Opportunities, like successes, don't have to be monumental in size; quite the opposite in fact. It's making small modifications to your strategy, products and services based on the small successes you noticed through any type of trending or feedback systems you use, that make the best changes. These are usually minor and thus offer minimum risk. Put together enough of these proven successful little wins and eventually you've developed a large, virtually risk free, successful product or service.

This concept is at the very heart of Japanese Management philosophy.

Do we have a stable Opportunity funding-model that doesn't fluctuate with our internal economic cycles?

When times get hard, cut back. Big Mistake! Oh, of course if your company is in jeopardy of financial collapse it is obvious to cut your opportunity spending, but otherwise there should be a separate fund and separate method of accounting for the ongoing tracking and exploitation of opportunities. This is even more important in economic hard times as unknowledgeable competition will likely cut back on opportunity funding and miss upcoming opportunities or not take advantage of known opportunities which you can then take advantage of.

What should our organizational structure be?

This depends on what you are trying to achieve *at this moment*. What I mean is that there is no perfect organizational structure. One model doesn't fit all. Knowledge workers require teams. Laborers may best be suited to classic hierarchy reporting systems. It really depends on what this particular group of individuals is trying to accomplish that should dictate the structure. Carefully outlining all the projects, sub projects, processes and tasks will create logical divisions in the enterprise and will provide a visual representation of the preferred reporting systems based on the current projects at this specific moment in time. As projects and processes change, so should the reporting structure.

How can we eliminate the middleman in knowledge exchange?

"For each person that a piece of information must travel through, the noise doubles and the value is cut in half". Therefore we need to create real-time face-to-face communication mechanisms.

How do we reward participation in knowledge exchange?

Read Chapter 6

How much are knowledge workers worth?

Read Chapter 10

Who should succeed whom, when and how?

An interesting concept! Most companies don't have a succession system so instead they breed a lot of internal political jockeying and infighting to curry favor and get next in line. Not only that but senior executives also don't typically address who will take their place in sufficient time to successfully transfer their skills and knowledge to their successor. This leaves the successor having to re-invent the wheel over and over. Companies should look at formal successor programs.

How do we build an environment to support knowledge workers?

Read Chapter 6

How are we planning on dealing with the aging worker population?

Companies *must* put into place programs that are designed to provide adult educational services to existing staff. They need to develop programs that deal with retiring knowledge workers and encourage them to stay-on in one form or another. Perhaps they can work a few days a week, just mornings, 3 months on 3 months off. There is likely to be a multitude of different packages that must be offered, as each knowledge worker will have individual requirements at that stage of their life. We cannot be lax in the development and testing of these programs. The companies that can grasp the magnitude of importance of this issue and can prepare to properly manage this issue will succeed. Other companies, basing their business strategy on knowledge workers, that don't prepare for the management of aging knowledge workers, will struggle or fail.

How do we train our employees?

Knowledge workers *MUST* have a constant stream of upgrade training. Not just to keep their skills current, but also because the fundamental nature of their personalities requires constant mental stimulation. Serious long-term programs MUST be put in place.

Do we have our best people assigned to opportunities or to problem solving?

Here is another topic worthy of focusing a monitoring strategy upon. Our tendency is to always send our top guns in to solve problems. These are usually the best thinkers and strategists. The problem with that approach is that the majority of the time the problem exists within an existing product, service or process. The product, service or process is considered important to the company so they want it repaired. This principle is a big mistake. The product, service or process is typically important because it already has an established market, service-base, revenue stream and so on. The number one task a company should be performing is finding new opportunities for growth. Therefore, these top guns, the best of the best, should be directing their full attention to opening new growth opportunities for the company within the realm of the corporate strategy, not fixing problems with existing products, services or processes.

Do we regularly target improvements to our products and services both upstream and down?

What does it cost to produce your widget? Are you aware of your supplier and distributor cost structures, quality assurance procedures and profit margins? Are you aware of their entire downstream supplier cost structures, quality assurance procedures and profit margins? Are you aware of your upstream distributors cost structures, customer perceptions, service capabilities, profit margins, abandoning strategies, marketing strategies and branding strategy? Are you aware of how every aspect of the above affects the price and quality of your final product or service?

You should develop programs that regularly test the complete upstream/downstream validity model. This should happen at least annually and require each upstream/downstream associate to increase their quality and decrease their costs by a *fixed* percentage every year.

Are we providing our knowledge workers with information or just data?

Data is everywhere and is completely useless. Until someone applies knowledge to the data and puts it into context in doesn't become information. Both too much data and too much information is also useless because humans just won't take the time to digest too much information to deliver a decision or take action. We need to filter, localize and qualify the information that is delivered to knowledge workers.

What constitutes a test of our organizational health?

A balance sheet is good, but not good enough. We need to be able to develop a test that encapsulates our entire deliverable as an enterprise, end-to-end. This starts with our customer's assessment of our value and better yet what our non-customers assess our value at. This test would go upstream and down and would model a complete multi-dimensional vision of our position, our competitors positions, the market position, the economic position and the political position.

How can I transfer my knowledge?

You need to transfer the knowledge out of your head and into others or it's useless to the company. I know a very brilliant man that can't articulate himself very well and confuses everyone when he speaks. He may be brilliant but he's an uncharted island, and uncharted islands of knowledge are of no value to anyone if you can't find them.

What information do I need?

Knowledge management is the future, but only for those that know what they want and what they need. These wants and needs must be clearly articulated or no one will be able to give the required information to you without a lot of guessing and that leads to critical errors in judgment.

How will our KMS question knowledge workers assumptions?

The hat is empty, I can see inside it. Yet when I reach inside I pull out a rabbit. Not only was I wrong but also it's completely illogical to actually find a rabbit in the hat as that is not a rabbit's normal habitat. Time and time again we assume that something will be a certain way because that is what *should* happen. We need to constantly test these assumptions and test the decisions that are made. Only through testing and the provision of supporting evidence, logical reasoning, and the process of risk elimination can we gain any confidence in our strategy.

How do we present the same information in different perspectives to support different purposes?

Cost accounting is one small piece of a much larger jigsaw puzzle. When we pull together a cross section of information it will be interpreted in different ways by different people. Some people are assigned the task to cut costs and others are assigned the tasks of exploring new opportunities. We both require the same information pulled in from the same departments but knowledge workers are going to look for different opportunities in each area in order to achieve different results. We want to store the information once but present many configurable views into the information.

At what point does information require action?

There's a car coming towards you and you're walking across the middle of the road. Your brain quickly rationalizes that, with the car moving the speed it's moving, you've got X amount of time before you get hit. Now you have to make decisions: move, get hit, or hope the driver stops in time

The car is getting too close now (the THRESHOLD) so you decide to jump out of the way.

But then your ex-wife suddenly shows up (the EVENT) on the opposite side of the road. This suddenly encourages you to frighten the driver into swerving out of control to your ex-wife's side of the road.

At some point in time the information we are presented with can be used to test against predetermined thresholds and events. Provided we don't exceed the thresholds we predetermined, or certain events do or don't take place, then we can proceed. If a threshold is passed or an event takes place we can initiate an action. Technology is a great tool for automating these monitoring functions.

One study has shown that the volume of information the world is being assaulted with doubles every 5 years and that we have created more information in the past 10 years than we have created throughout the entire history of mankind.

We need to start developing extensive filters that are built to trigger on events and thresholds. The human body has five senses (six if you watch the movies). The human eye alone presents our brain with an estimated 250 million bits of information every second. So how is it that, with such an astronomical amount of data pouring into our brain, we are still able to notice the small coin in the grass at the side of the walkway?

We can pick out the coin because we have built in filters that establish what is the norm and what falls outside the norm. Anything that falls outside of our "normal" filter breeches a threshold that triggers and event in our brain. These are the types of systems that knowledge management intends to create throughout the automated environment of an organization.

How can we filter useless data?

See Chapter 5

External Information

Business now dominates politics. Geographical borders are invisible to organizational structure today and in the foreseeable future, which means that organizational concerns start taking preference over political concerns. No longer do we or will we build private infrastructures for each country that we spread our business wings into. We will continue to capitalize on centralized manufacturing, support functions and financing. We will need to engage knowledge workers on a global basis to assimilate the most accurate information and the most innovative ideas, not only from our own knowledge staff, but also from every partner, customer and supplier.

We not only need to track information we know we need, we also have to monitor information about outside influences that could potentially impact our strategies from areas we know nothing about or have any influence on. In other words we need to also be monitoring for things that don't exist today but might show up tomorrow and things that exist but we don't know about yet.

For example, telecommunication carriers that make the bulk of their profits from long-distance services had best not just concern themselves with their immediate competition. They need to study the impact of sending telephone calls over the Internet, which bypasses their toll systems.

How many buggy manufacturers survived the invention of the horseless carriage by converting their buggy bodies to automobile bodies? Answer: None. Outside influences present the greatest threat and opportunities to organizations of tomorrow and knowledge management is the early warning system. Therefore, cultivation of knowledge management systems that capture external information is essential to success in every organization.

How well have our results matched our customer's expectations?

The customer is our market and the market moves to the product or service offering the perception of the greatest value. It doesn't matter whether the market is growing, mature or declining from the perspective of measuring our results. Businesses can make profit in any of the three markets, it only matters whether or not our results match those desired by the consumer. If they don't match then we have trouble with our strategy.

Were the successes planned for or were they side effects?

It is an important distinction between success attributed to strategic planning and success attributed to luck. Any success outside of our planned expectations means we have trouble with our strategy or our ability to strategize. Even small successes outside of the scope of our plan can point to significant shifts in the market attitude, the maturation or decline of a product or service or the potential of a new growth area. It also means we don't have the information we need or the skills we need to assess our own market. In any respect, the monitoring and analyzing of all successes is actually more important than the reverse, the analyzing of failures. Don't get me wrong, analyzing failures is important as well but I don't believe it as important as analyzing successes. Be safe, do both.

Did our successes align with our business philosophy?

If we do achieve success outside the scope of our strategy, it could point us into new growth areas. It's then that we need to carefully assess if the new growth areas align with our business philosophy. We need to make very important decisions at this point. Is our philosophy wrong? Does it need changing? Is the existing market changing? Is this new market a formal swing or just a fad?

What opportunities did we miss?

We need to recognize opportunities when they show themselves. More importantly we need to take advantage of them. We need to track and analyze missed opportunities. Did we not have the skills to take advantage of the opportunities? Did we miss it entirely? Are our processes for monitoring potential opportunities defective?

Were we able to turn our opportunities and successes into a viable product?

I have a good example of turning opportunities into products from when I started working with Omni Technology Centers in Atlanta. I was brought in to develop and coordinate the infrastructure department development efforts. I was still in the initial stages when we picked up on an opportunity to get in with Microsoft on the early developmental stages of Windows 2000, Microsoft's next generation NT operating system. When I had a hard look at the initial alpha product I could see how this new version of the famous operating system was so much more powerful for programmers than previous and current versions.

Omni's current business philosophy was to build software applications for Internet enabled commerce based on the COM specifications (a very focused strategy). I gathered together the fragmented employees that specialized in infrastructure and built a team to dissect this new product offering and learn everything we could about it. I basically pulled everyone off their current work and had them focus intimately on the various subsystems and come to the table for knowledge transfer sessions and to debate the merits of this and that. More than the product itself, this was the first time these employees had seriously engaged in a team effort focused on knowledge transfer (at least at Omni). They had each primarily done their own thing up to then and were comfortable with that. Suddenly, we had built a very cohesive work unit completely targeted on a specific objective. Our combined strength became apparent to everyone and before long even Microsoft held our team in high regard as being one of the foremost experts on their newest addition to their operating system family, in that geographical region.

While we were performing our research we documented all our findings and built and tested training materials still in their infant stages. When our research project was complete, not only was our team able to begin supporting our developer community but we where able to spawn off the processes and documents we created as additional projects. Primarily it provided plenty of background to enable Omni to begin offering formal Windows 2000 training courses prior to the competition.

Another opportunity that presented itself as a side effect of the research was the development of the OmniNET knowledge base concept. Even as I write, the OmniNET knowledge base is a rapidly growing structured and unstructured knowledge repository that is fully accessible across the Internet so that all the Omni engineers on customer sites, hiding behind complex firewalls, can still get access to the complete OmniNET knowledge management system. The initial test knowledgebase was built on top of Windows 2000 to test its functionality and interoperability. We wound up removing Windows 2000 because it was still not stable enough for production at that time but the knowledge base concept grew and grew and was moved into production shortly after the release of Office 2000.

This high-energy infrastructure team tested, documented, broke and fixed the test product. At the end of three months we were ready to support our development team. Even more than that, we had implemented a new project management framework and come ahead with an extremely confident and innovative infrastructure team which is opening new opportunities for the development teams everyday because of the project exposure.

In summary we could sense one opportunity and were able to turn it into a multitude of new service offerings and new internal processes. More than we could have anticipated going into the venture.

How much are customers willing to pay?

There was a time when we could add up all our costs to deliver a product or service, market it up X number of points, and sell it. Oh well, those days are pretty much gone. Now we have to find out what the customers are willing to pay and work backwards. We need to use the sell price to dictate all of our downstream costing. Therefore, as you can see, intimate knowledge about how our customer relates value of our product or service to a mental purchase price they are willing to pay gives us the viability test we need on an on-going basis.

Is a product or service we offer growing, mature or declining?

If it's growing, watch your risks. If it's mature, watch your costs. If it's declining, strategically abandon it. The key to this issue is truly knowing which of the markets you're really in, which is one of the things that catches too many companies.

Are we gaining an increasing share of a decreasing market?

If you're in a decreasing market and you're picking up more and more share of the market then you're going to be in for a big surprise one day soon. Best to perform some homework on where your customers are going and why.

I like to talk about the advent of the automobile and it's impact on the horse and buggy industry. Picture the buggy whip manufacturers. I bet that by the time the last of the buggies were being sold, the last remaining buggy whip manufacturer was the one that made the very best buggy whip, and was picking up more market share every day. Unfortunately, there is a foregone future for all companies that live in a declining market.

What upstream and downstream information do I need?

Total end-to-end quality and performance assurance accounting information is required to get true insight into the validity of the company, the market and the strategy.

What performance levels do we need to achieve?

Remember that the job of management is to achieve results and performance. Define the metrics you expect in your strategy and factor the thresholds. Use the thresholds as triggers to warn of pending trouble. Thresholds and events are effective, as they act as filters to keep management from being overwhelmed by to much data. The problem can occur when the thresholds are set wrong and troubles can start without the alarms going off.

How do we measure our performance?

There are always internal measurements but until you measure yourself against the competition you don't have anything. You need to track how well or poorly the competition is doing and determine why. You need to measure their growth, market share and strategies. You need to compare them against your own and find and expose every success you can discern from the competition and capitalize on it. The same goes for their failures. You're now doing it internally, now it's time to do it externally.

What demographics will affect us?

The one biggest demographic factor that will affect you will be changes in disposable income.

With the declining birthrate in developed countries we will soon see the bulk of disposable income in the hands of those nearing or entered into retirement. Gone are the yuppies of the 80's and they are continuing to decline. As the crowd with the cash gets older, so also their ideals and values change. Conservative becomes the key word, which is even better for the booming financial investment sector. We will see gradual shifts in all markets over the next 25 years.

Not the best of times to think about going into the snowboard manufacturing business. If this book makes me enough money I'd probably buy a cruise line.

What economic shifts will affect us?

The collapse of the Asian monetary system was a bad thing don't you think. It's small things like that that should be monitored. Actually, a lot of knowledge-based companies that knew what to look for predicted the pending disaster well prior to the collapse. So it goes to show you that a good knowledge management system can potentially save your company from disaster.

What political shifts can affect us?

Economic shifts usually impact organizations over longer periods of time than political shifts.

I owned a company that was the best of the best in communications in a small market. I won all the major gravy contracts, which were all for the government of course. I won the first large contract for one government agency and everything was good. The reputation we picked up was spread through word of mouth amongst all the government agencies until I had absorbed all the local government business. Now things were great. My competition was not the least bit pleased and had to settle for second choice pickings in the private sector, and I was very happy. Nothing could go wrong.

Nothing, except an election of course. I felt we were so entrenched in the government that I never paid it sufficient attention. For that matter they were even providing my entire company with office space inside their buildings just to keep us to themselves.

After the election, the *other* guys got in. I still didn't pay much attention because our allies were the 30-year guys and nothing was going to happen to them, right? Well, at first nothing happened. Then came the day of reckoning when all the government's departmental CEO's and CFO's were replaced with "politically friendly" CEO's and CFO's. Suddenly, overnight, the tides of power had changed and of course everything the previous CEO's and CFO's had done was horribly wrong according to the new regime. It wasn't long after when the contracts started drying up and funding was cut or redirected elsewhere.

Now I had a problem. I had to go out into the real world to make a living now. I was packing an excellent reputation after having done the biggest of the biggest and being the best of the best. So I figured this was no problem, right?

Wrong. Even though my company seriously outclassed the competition, while I was enjoying the fruits of an isolated world my competition had developed a solid footing through-out private enterprise. They weren't as good, and they didn't have the reputation, but they were now *proven*. I had thrown them the table scraps and completely misread the power of the political environment and what impact it could have on my company. Had I been oh so much wiser, I would have diversi-fied into the private sector to a much greater extent.

Meanwhile, the competition, being too weak to even realize it, had built a much stronger marketing model because I let them, through my own bad strategizing. My only saving grace was the deep branding I'd generated. I was able to pen-etrate deep enough to ride out the political storm, but I would never, ever allow myself to get caught believing my market is indestructible again.

How will global currency exchange fluctuations affect us?

This is becoming more prevalent and will continue to do so. We have to be carefully aware of currency fluctuations and the only real way we can control this is through a central facility that tracks all the currencies. Global companies are moving to central currency systems to help protect themselves from global currency gyrations. But even local companies are affected by fluctuations in local currency, like the massive hit local businesses took in Malaysia when the Malaysian currency plummeted.

What do we need to be globally competitive?

We now have to monitor competition and emerging technologies on a global basis, not just local, even if we only do business locally right now.

There was a company I helped out for a while that designed and installed microwave and communication systems. They brought me in because needed help in re-engineering their internal and external processes. While I was there it became obvious that they had grown very comfortable in their respective geographical region. They spent the time analyzing the competition in their region and offered the best compensation packages in the local industry. They hired very good engineers and presented a very decent work environment. They would meet and discuss their risks of losing personnel and market share. It looked on the surface that everything was being accounted for.

Unfortunately, it wasn't long after I had started that calls started coming in for engineers that offered them double what they were making and all expenses paid for one year. *In Malaysia!* Shortly there after, Malaysia airlines was filling their seats with bodies that used to fill the seats all around me.

There was a period of frustration and service suffered, but in the end the engineers came back after their stint in sunnier climates, and they were taken back in without hesitation. After all, you can't really control knowledge workers, just present them with opportunities.

The bottom line is, that competition can and will come from everywhere.

What is our non-competition up to?

We always have to keep an eye out for our close neighbors and sometimes distant cousins that just might accidentally bump into or attract our existing market. Remember those good old 8 tracks and LP's? I bet you those manufacturers are still trying to figure out how one's and zero's can be music on digital CD's.

How do we benchmark against the competition?

We always need to know where we stand because if we're not first, or at least tied for first place then we are not as competitive, and not capitalizing on what our competition is doing right. You should always be able to do at least everything your competition does that proves successful.

What has our competition succeeded or failed at and why?

I can't state enough that you need a knowledge pipeline into your competitors so you can capitalize on every single one of their successes that fit into your business philosophy. You also need to learn from their mistakes as it saves you an awful lot of money and time.

What outside technologies can affect us?

Who ever thought that cars would replace horses or that Paul Bunyan would lose to a chainsaw? Imagine that. You must watch out for alternate technologies as they truly provide opportunity for a larger threat than your visible competition. In one of my first companies, I specialized in communication cabling. The competition was installing coaxial and shielded cable at the time and the competition was fairly strong in the form of electrical contractors. New technologies developed that allowed transmission of high-speed computer signals over ordinary cheap telephone wires and came available in the form of special adapters. They originated in the telecommunications market, not the electrical market.

Over night I locked up the market by picking up the distribution rights on the only available products at that time. I began chasing the biggest contracts that the competition had a solid foothold in, and came in well under the combined parts and labor bids of the competition because they didn't have a comparable, cost effective offering. I could bid under them comfortably in the products area and maintain huge profit margins in both labor and parts. I maintained that advantage for quite a while. It didn't last forever, nothing does, but the fact remains that these electrical contractors were just plain blind-sided by a completely new technology. They were so busy studying each other and competing for the best prices on the same materials they didn't watch the world evolving outside their private markets. I must admit, I most definitely took great pleasure in that conquest. When they finally got their hands on competitive products and started to erode the margins, I was already long gone into Fiber Optics leaving them another couple of years behind.

What policies should be in place to manage external change?

Change is the one constant. You can either fear it or ride with it. The one thing you can't do is "manage change". But you can create it, which offers you more control than leaving things to the wiles of nature, but you run higher risk. But then again, can you risk not to risk? At least if you choose to just monitor it you can perhaps receive advance warning and your staff will get acclimatized to constant interaction with change. Change management (the concept, not the process) is a particularly mythological beast and I don't want to get into it here.

What is our image to our customers?

We always have to obtain regular feedback as to the image we're presenting to our clients. Once we have learned what our clients truly value then we need to present (or at the very least, create the perception) that we offer what they need or want. If we get lazy then we get like a really, really big computer mainframe manufacturer I know that also made typewriters a long time ago. They got so arrogant that customers detested them. They had a virtual monopoly for a while but you all know that monopolies don't last. When competitive products arrived, clients abandoned ship at the speed of light. They've spent many years trying to reclaim a little ground that they're not big and evil, but that is just marketing fluff. They still are big and evil deep down. Their top management must be blind if they haven't noticed their company shrinking like Rick Moranis' kids.

What type of branding should we have to match the market?

You need to brand your company if you intend to live though the trends and cycles. That big company I just mentioned above, they have a brand. Even if they produced a piece of junk it would probably still sell for a while just because of the reputation associated with that brand. Branding adds incredible weight to your battleship. That way if you have engine difficulty or have to ram into your competition, it's going to take and awful lot to stop your momentum.

Knowing what we now know, is there a better way?

Continually ask yourself this question. Let's assume you make green widgets. You've been making them for a few years now and they sell. If you were to get into the same product again, now knowing what you know, would you manufacture, distribute and sell them the same way you are now? If the answer is no then you better go back to your strategy because you have a problem. You should visit this question on everything you do or produce on a regularly programmed cycle, at least once a year.

Let's use an example by saying that you sell toys. Ten years ago you opened your first store and since then you've opened twenty more. You've now also invested in a central warehouse and you're spending lots of time and money tracking inventory control, staffing issues, and all the other baggage that comes with being in the retail business.

Now you sit down at your next strategy meeting and ask everyone a question;

The question is *"If we new that the Internet would be as big as it is today, and we could have planned for it and sold all our toys across the internet, shipped direct from the manufacturer to the client, carried no inventory and had no store fronts, then spend all our marketing dollars getting clients to visit a web site, would we be doing business the way we are now?"*

If you say that you would have gone in the direction of the Internet strategy, then you need to revisit your current strategy and determine whether or not you're pushing a rope instead of pulling it.

How do we present the same information in different perspectives to support different purposes?

> We need to create multiple views of our information so we can see our information at work in different contexts. This allows us to apply different knowledge to the same information to test for potentially different outcomes. If I'm in marketing or sales, I want to see our information presented from the perspective of creating wealth. If I'm in accounting I want to see the same information presented in the form of asset preservation. We see two completely different objectives and perspectives but the same information.

How can we filter useless data?

> See Chapter 5

The Knowledge Environment

Everything dealing with knowledge management begins with culture. We must first gain a definitive understanding of the current attitudes of staff to sharing knowledge. Many organizations experience a prevalent attitude that knowledge is sacred to job security. This attitude is destructive to knowledge management and presents the single most significant hurdle to building a successful knowledge management system.

An important step in any knowledge management venture is to ensure the cooperation of the participants and instill the perceived value of shared knowledge. This is a huge undertaking in most enterprises but is directly related to the quality, quantity and integrity of the information in the knowledgebase. This cultural re-engineering effort usually demonstrates maximum return on Tacit knowledge. Explicit knowledge dissemination can usually be mandated as part of an employees base job description but Tacit knowledge has to be applied for. You can't get something from someone if you don't know it exists and they don't want you to have it. The participants must feel there is value to themselves personally if they contribute personal knowledge.

Knowledge is a precious commodity and individuals don't typically give away a precious possession, they sell it. In our everyday lives we gain in knowledge and share the knowledge when we feel it is personally advantageous to do so. Internally we put a value on the knowledge and we mentally wait until the bid price is right before selling. The price could be recognition, money, survival or building credit but there is always a price.

The heart of managing Tacit knowledge is building an environment that recognizes that Tacit knowledge comes with a price and builds into itself the vehicle for trade. This may encompass recognition programs and financial rewards but also generates a certain level of trust that compensation will be accounted for in one form or another. With mechanisms in place to broker knowledge it is much more likely to attract participants, which are crucial to success.

Assuming that you are a genius at human resource management and can solve the primary problem of cultural negotiation then you can target the technology, which is simple in comparison.

Now that we have a definition of knowledge management we need to move to the next step that requires the categorization of knowledge into logical groupings. This means that we need to decide where the knowledge is, what type of knowledge it is and who needs this knowledge.

The Process for Managing Tacit Knowledge

When we talk about information in the context of the business environment there is a tendency to think in terms of facts and figures, reports and statements, printouts or whatever appears on our computer terminal. It is relatively easy to obtain this type of information, which may be generated as a by-product of formal systems and processes already in place. While these forms of information are important, there are other forms, less formal, which can also play an important role in the decision making process.

Previous research has shown that the informal channels for collecting, what is termed, 'soft' information can be very important, particularly in more senior positions within the organization. Indeed, less regard is likely to be given to Explicit factual information. This tends to reflect the way in which managers work in the real world, where informal Tacit information (over the telephone or in the lunchroom) is collected and stored until other items of information (either Tacit or Explicit) reinforce or add to that information, like pieces in a jig-saw puzzle. The human mind is extremely effective at this form of 'information management' far more so than computers, where attempts to mirror this methodology have been relatively unsuccessful.

An important aspect of a knowledge management system (KMS) is its potential to not only focus on Explicit information and associated systems but also to assist in development and nurturing the informal contacts and networks that operate in and between organizations.

Consider the following diagram:

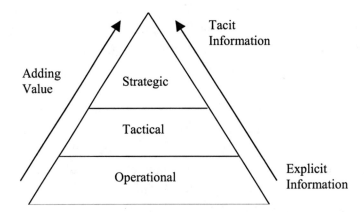

When we begin associating a value on our knowledge we can begin to realize that Tacit knowledge holds greater value to an enterprise than Explicit knowledge. Because of the complexities of collecting and managing Tacit data, the cost of developing and deploying a knowledgebase built for Tacit knowledge is likely to exceed that of an Explicit knowledgebase. However the return on long-term investment should be greater for a Tacit knowledgebase than and Explicit knowledgebase.

Consider the distinctions between `Tacit' and `Explicit' Knowledge. Tacit knowledge is described as personal context-specific and therefore hard to formalize and communicate. Explicit knowledge refers to knowledge that is transmittable in formal, systematic language. The distinction between the two is extremely important—for example, the delayering of organizations in the 70's and 80's viewed middle managers as conveyors of explicit information between layers of the organization, something which new technology, in particular `networks`, could supplant. However, many organizations failed to take account of the Tacit knowledge of these managers—something that subsequently created major problems for many of them.

Culturally we begin with the creation of a "knowledge map" that identifies what people know and how we can approach them. The process I use is called HELP (Heuristic Enterprise Learning Program), which will be discussed in Chapter 6.

Once we understand who are the holders of specific knowledge then our job is to build infrastructure to support face-to-face communications with the least amount of effort. We can provide technologies to facilitate text-based conversations but the subtle nuances of facial movements and vocal intonations often carry significant translation of information and provide substance to knowledge we lose in other mediums.

Face-to-Face communications also enhances the level of trust required to broker precious information. Knowing that a piece of knowledge, transferred to text may be replicated anywhere, for free, offers a barrier to participation. As I spoke of earlier, knowledge participants need to broker their knowledge for a variety of reasons. Face-to-Face communications offers the constructive environment for negotiation.

The Process for Managing Explicit Knowledge

Technologically, we will start by identifying current physical repositories of knowledge. Physical knowledge stores will usually include file servers, databases, messaging systems, Internet/Intranet/Extranet web sites, accounting systems, corporate libraries, etc.

Physical knowledge stores contain different types of knowledge management participants. For example a database will contain data. Raw data is useless until someone places it in context. Data in context becomes information. Information then needs to be evaluated, conclusions drawn and actions initiated. At the time that conclusions are drawn and action taken then information has been utilized in the knowledge process.

In essence, what I am saying is that knowledge, in the general sense, is really the rationalization we undergo before taking action on information.

Let's use an example. I hand you a sheet of paper with three numbers on it; $500, $200, and $50. Of what value is this to you? Not much, but this is data. Now let's wrap some context around this data and convert it to information by telling you these numbers represent the price of Microsoft shares for the next three days. Is this knowledge yet? No, this is information. What we do with this information requires knowledge. What action will you take as a result of this information? If you don't own Microsoft shares, you're going run out and sell Microsoft short for all your worth. But what about the person who owns Microsoft shares and bought them at $400? That person uses the same information but runs out and sells every Microsoft share they own, and fast. Two people applied their own personal knowledge to the information they were given.

Once we know where data, information and knowledge are stored we need to determine the context of the knowledge we want to assimilate into a system in order to convert data to information and information into knowledge. This process allows us to define whether the knowledge we wish to collect is local, regional, global, product specific, process specific, business unit specific, etc. There is little value in creating a huge centralized repository of indexed data if the resultant of a query produces 2 million responses. Sales information specific to weather conditions in Europe is of little value to people looking for sales information about a specific product in New York. Nobody will take the time to sort through such a large quantity of data to extract the tidbits of information they need to make decisions. It is the tendency of humans to take the fastest knowledge as opposed to the most qualified knowledge. Therefore our objective behind categorization is to place knowledge into a specific context that allows us to filter the knowledge based on relevance into logical units of work and present the most relevant knowledge first. The filtering mechanism used most often is called Meta data. Unfortunately, Meta data is not always available for us to use so we also need to utilize policy and technology to assimilate, filter and present relevant knowledge. We will talk about Meta data in greater detail Chapter 5.

After defining the type or classification of information we what to assimilate we need to go back to the repositories we identified earlier and determine a method of either indexing or extracting the information we require. Whether we index or extract is dependent on the structure in which the data resides. We typically index document and conversational (unstructured) data and extract database (structured) data. A search server usually provides the required indexing function. Extracted data from databases is usually consolidated into a data warehouse. The results of the analysis performed against a data warehouse can then be combined with the search server results and presented as a single portal view into the consolidated knowledge base.

Once we have defined the Explicit knowledge we wish to collect, identified the resources that can supply the data, developed the methodology to assimilate the data into a collective framework we can then begin the task of writing programs that can provide analysis of the data and continue to present different views of the information through the same portal front-end. The depth of analysis is dependent on the perceived value of the data. This can range from simple search results to data mining and neural networks. Specific tools to facilitate knowledge management will be discussed in Chapter 8.

Summary

The key to knowledge management is recognizing that we want to employ enterprise-wide change for the purpose of performance and innovation gains. Knowledge affects everyone and is therefore an excellent vehicle to facilitate change. Knowledge management should be a never-ending process and should be as fundamental in an enterprise as accounting. It is impossible to achieve total knowledge management as the target is forever moving. The infrastructure we can build to support knowledge management is tangible and deliverable and should be a mandate in every organization, large and small.

CHAPTER 2—
The Preliminary Research

Phase 1—The Research Map

The road to success begins with the first step. In this chapter we will outline the necessary steps to follow to begin collecting the information required to build a knowledge management system. Whether you desire to build a knowledgebase for Explicit or Tacit information you will need to follow this guideline as the preliminary information-gathering phase.

Please refer to the Research Map located at the end of this Chapter as your reference map.

Step 1 – Establish the definition of KM

Step 1—When starting your research efforts the first step is to define knowledge management. It is imperative that everyone concerned with the knowledge management effort has a common definition and vocabulary to provide a solid foundation for discourse. This includes the Board of Directors, as a knowledge initiative must have buy-in from the top. The most logical way to proceed would be to buy lots of additional copies of this book and hand them out (what else would you expect an author to say).

> **Step 2 –**   *Define the logical and physical corporate structure.*
> *Internal and External entities*

Step 2—You will need to map out the physical organization of the
enterprise. Geographies play a major part in collaboration and knowledge transfer. Geography influences both Tacit and Explicit knowledge
efforts as it affects awareness and access of knowledge resources as
well as requirements for communication infrastructure. Next we work
on gathering the logical structure of the enterprise. The logical structure is the departmentalization or categorization of the organization and
will potentially become the foundation for initial classification of both
Tacit and Explicit knowledge. It is most relevant to also collect the perceived utopian logical model, as there may be a hidden or expressed
desire to re-engineer the logical model. You must also collect the
rationale behind the potential re-engineering efforts to get a better
grasp of current perceived inefficiencies in the corporate structure.

> **Step 3 –**   *Define the existing corporate reporting structure.*

Step 3—You need to ascertain the existing corporate reporting structure, as these are the existing "hard coded" methods of communication
and escalation. These may play a significant or minor part in the
knowledge flow through an enterprise but the use of titles is often
accredited with the identification of specific repositories of knowledge. There may be no validity to the claim that someone is knowledgeable about what is described in their title or in their willingness to
participate in knowledge transfer but at this stage you can take nothing
for granted.

Step 4 –   *Determine perceived KM problems from the Board*

Step 4—It is crucial at this juncture that the topmost officials in the organization define for you what they perceive are the inefficiencies in knowledge management in their organization. This information is critical to the formulation of the Vision Statement. These problems will be the motivators, both financially and organizationally for the KM project. The knowledge management effort must be bound back to and measured against the problems it is intended to rectify. Throughout the life of this project you will always be returning to the vision statement to test yourself and the nature of your deliverables. Any deviation from the vision statement must be forwarded to the knowledge management steering committee or whatever similar body is established; through proper change management initiatives that are in place, to maintain the scope of the KM project.

Step 5 –   *Determine what they perceive as the utopian KM model for their company*

Step 5—You must now ascertain, from the senior most officials, what they perceive is the utopian knowledge management environment for the enterprise. Do not limit this discussion to the specific scope of this particular KM initiative, you will need a broad sweeping picture of the long term goals of the enterprise towards knowledge management in general to make sure that your initiative is in synchronization with the long-term vision. You will eventually need to drill down to specifics about this particular project to define the scope, timeline and budget (the Trinity of project management). This effort should take into account any efforts the organization is making now and in the future for internal, external and interorganizational knowledge transfer. It is also relevant at this stage to ascertain whether or not there are particular components of the internal organization or entities outside the organization that they intend to merge, separate, sell or acquire in the near future.

| *Step 6 – Determine their existing project management framework* |

Step 6—It is important in this step to determine if they have an enterprise model for project management. A project management framework will be providing their organization with an enterprise scale knowledge delivery mechanism that can be capitalized on for not only deploying this particular KM venture but as a wealth of knowledge resources and knowledge flow patterns. Project management is specifically designed to offer structure to knowledge and structure to reporting mechanisms, which will encompass risk, opportunity, issue and change management. These functions of project management are significant repositories and processes for dealing with Tacit knowledge. The project document stores are excellent repositories of Explicit knowledge. Finally, if the project management framework exists, it is an excellent, if not mandatory, vehicle for deploying your own KM initiative.

| *Step 7 – Determine what technologies they leverage on behalf of KM* |

Step 7—Determine what, if any, knowledge management specific technologies are in use at the moment or projected. Significant historical research in tools for KM is usual in most organizations because it is the most widely publicized component of knowledge management. The organization may also have already undertaken knowledge management initiatives in the past and may have failed or are currently using some methodology that they deem relevant to your current effort. If they have tried in the past and failed it is wise to expose the history at this stage and attempt to determine why the historic KM project failed or didn't produce the anticipated results. This information may provide valuable clues for successful completion of the current KM project.

Step 8 –   ***Determine current communications infrastructure***

Step 8—Due diligence is required on the entire communication infrastructure from LAN's, WAN's and MAN,s to protocols and technologies. In the instance where the KM project is focused on Tacit
knowledge, bandwidth between participants becomes the single most
significant factor. As I stated earlier, Tacit knowledge is best transferred
face-to-face, providing the mechanisms for knowledge brokering and
generating a trust level unattainable in text-based communications.
Tacit KM solutions will almost invariably wind up taking full advantage of communication technology focused on video conferencing and
collaboration. These applications are very bandwidth consumptive and
require robust network infrastructure and careful bandwidth planning.
Frequently, the IT section of an organization is delegated the responsibility to deliver KM projects, and the IT section almost invariably has
nothing to do with the telecommunications section. Delivery mechanisms for Tacit KM should account for all communication mediums
including the organizations telephone system(s) that are often designed
from the ground up to handle video conferencing demands. Other
aspects of delivery of video based communications could include
broadband transmission (Cable Television infrastructure), microwave
or satellite communications. All of these technologies must be considered as viable communication mediums with substantial differences in
delivery costs and functionality.

Step 9 –   ***Determine current work environment applications and
desktop/laptop configurations***

Step 9—Here we identify the desktop productivity tools currently in
use, identifying the type and versions prevalent throughout the enterprise. We also want to establish the lowest common denominator of
workstations and the current configurations (how much RAM on

machines, hard drive capacities, CPU speeds, level of graphics. etc.). Delivery of desktop components is the single most time consuming aspect of deployment. Knowledge management technologies for desktops (especially desktop video conferencing) can be very machine consumptive. Machines and desktop productivity tools may also present myriad operating systems and delivery applications as well as multiple versions and models. Standardization of desktop machines to participate in KM would be nice but not always within budget, timeline or feasibility if machines are deployed around specific mission-critical business application requirements. This information is crucial to determine the true cost of deployment, as this is typically the most expensive aspect of deployment. Modifying user workstations also has dramatic effect of visual impact to the user community and the need for additional end-user training. Mobile users present problems of their own, often limited in available bandwidth and by security concerns, all of which must be calculated into the risk analysis and funding model for the project.

Step 10 –   ***Determine current messaging platforms***

Step 10—Determine the nature and extent of existing messaging platforms. Messaging platforms include both the tradition e-mail systems as well as application messaging (such as Microsoft's MSMQ). Messaging systems play an important role in knowledge management as they provide an efficient form of alternate asynchronous communication, which is conducive to workflow knowledge management. Messaging in the form of e-mail is a rapidly expanding force in today's communication infrastructure but provides two significant barriers in knowledge management. The first problem with e-mail is that it provides little or no opportunity to facilitate the brokering of knowledge. Once someone has documented a piece of valuable knowledge then, once transmitted, is available for public broadcast and dissemination. Once knowledge is passed on it is perceived to diminish in value to the originator and therefore offers a psychological roadblock to knowledge transfer. The second problem with e-mail is that people rarely desire to broadcast that they don't know something. Once a piece of knowledge is documented and broadcast it is now Explicit and can and should be continually challenged to provide further validation. People don't typically enjoy being proven wrong and therefore are frequently reluctant to pass along a piece of interpolative information, which is at the heart of Tacit or innovative knowledge.

Step 11 –	***Determine current types of data storage systems Intranet/Internet/Extranet***

Step 11—In this step we attempt to understand and locate data repositories and existing applications that can provide the data framework and tools for our KM undertaking.

Data stores mainly consist of:

1. Databases, Data Warehouses, Accounting systems
2. Groupware or Collaboration software
3. Messaging systems
4. Web software
5. ERP software
6. EIS software
7. Business Process Automation Software
8. E-Commerce Software
9. Search Software
10. PIM software

> *Step 12 –*   ***Determine location of current repositories (internal and***
> ***External)***
> ***Structured, unstructured and workflow***

Step 12—After identifying the types of data repositories we need to now identify the location of the repositories. This process usually consists of identifying the physical location, make, model and configurations of Mainframe computers, File and Application servers. It is a good idea to identify the network segments and available bandwidth into each device as KM tools can often significantly load and tax existing network and server infrastructure. Eventually we will need to estimate the potential demands that will be placed on each device and determine if network or system upgrades are required to facilitate the KM demands.

> *Step 13 –*   ***Determine current security model***

Step 13—Security concerns are or should be prevalent in any information system and communication network. Considering that we are dealing with one of the most significant aspects in any organization (knowledge) we must articulate that security should be even more significant an effort in this situation. A careful review of the existing security policies, processes and methodology is required at this stage. At this point we are not debating security but simply collecting the information with regards to existing security model.

> *Step 14 –*   ***Determine requirements for personalization and***
> ***membership***

Step 14—This step is the determination of the organizations need for personalization and membership. You may ask just what this has to do with knowledge management but the fact is that managing knowledge has many different aspects. In some cases, the management of knowledge may require the management of client or user information to provide services such as retrieval of personal information each time a user enters a system (even the knowledge management system) or the delivery of a common intake system to reduce redundancy in enterprise data. All of these things come together to make knowledge collection and transfer as simple as possible to encourage user participation. Personalization and membership is a viable component in the KM saga.

Step 15 – *Determine current directory services*

Step 15—Most organizations have many directory structures. From e-mail directories to Network logon directories to corporate telephone directories. The question is not whether they have a directory; the question is more of how many directories and of what type and structure. Consolidating directory structures is a significant and rewarding undertaking, providing a point of common data across the enterprise and providing end users and programmers with a central repository of common data. An enterprise directory facilitates significant consolidation of programming efforts and common data input/output for everyone and every application in the organization.

Step 16 – *Summarize your finding and get sign-off*

Step 16—Once you have collected the research information it is now time to consolidate your findings in a document and present the current state-of-affairs to the powers that be for sign-off and approval. After you get the green light on the current situation you now move to the next task of crafting the project Vision Statement, which is no small undertaking. Congratulate yourself on making it this far as you've probably turned over many stones and consumed many hours

from people that all thought they are too busy to take the time you really needed. The point is, if you didn't complete this phase of the project then there is no need to proceed to the next phase because of the near certainty of failure.

Research Map:

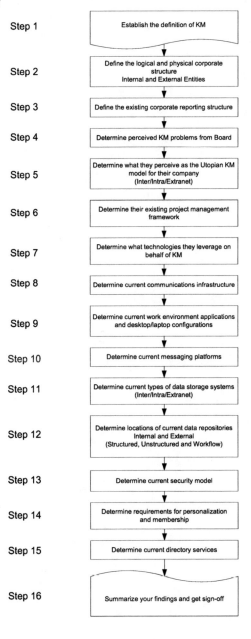

Step 1	Establish the definition of KM
Step 2	Define the logical and physical corporate structure Internal and External Entities
Step 3	Define the existing corporate reporting structure
Step 4	Determine perceived KM problems from Board
Step 5	Determine what they perceive as the Utopian KM model for their company (Inter/Intra/Extranet)
Step 6	Determine their existing project management framework
Step 7	Determine what technologies they leverage on behalf of KM
Step 8	Determine current communications infrastructure
Step 9	Determine current work environment applications and desktop/laptop configurations
Step 10	Determine current messaging platforms
Step 11	Determine current types of data storage systems (Inter/Intra/Extranet)
Step 12	Determine locations of current data repositories Internal and External (Structured, Unstructured and Workflow)
Step 13	Determine current security model
Step 14	Determine requirements for personalization and membership
Step 15	Determine current directory services
Step 16	Summarize your findings and get sign-off

CHAPTER 3—
Crafting a Vision Statement

Crafting a vision statement is critical to any projects success, not just a knowledge management project. Without a clearly articulated objective then there is little or no way to judge your direction or measure your success. "A ship afloat at sea" would be a good metaphor for those unwilling to describe, in writing, the project goals.

The more detailed we can articulate a vision statement the less room for misinterpretation. As we begin crafting we should consider the intended audience. This type of vision statement is designed as a position statement for organizational knowledge management and will have a far reaching and opinionated audience. Therefore each part of the vision should synchronize with the existing culture, the perceived future culture, the current business plan and the organizations marketing plan.

Knowledge management is a suite of pervasive support functions and is therefore a means to an end, not an end unto itself. A careful review of the organizational vision must be incorporated into the KM vision statement. This vision can be crafted by anyone with the ambition to undertake the research but the product of the statement must be acknowledged, agreed to and advertised by the Board of Directors or organization head. A vision imposed by a sub agency, department or section will cause potential political unrest as there will be a perceived shift in power because, as Francis Bacon states "knowledge is power" and people will react according to their perceived diminished value.

I recently wrote a vision statement for a Governor in the Midwest. I started with an articulate description of our objectives so as to eliminate many days of potential debate over interpretation. I was sitting in a position of authority in one particular department of the state government. I carefully weighed the cultural and technological aspects of the different agencies and put pen to paper to craft what I thought was a well versed technological direction for statewide common intake. I submitted the vision to the department head who immediately sliced, diced and watered down the goals. I was disappointed but could live with the resultant deliverable. From there it went to the Chief of Staff who proceeded to virtually cut it in half the "cleansed" statement and made the resulting vision so generic it could be interpreted in literally any way anyone decided. This is of course, what the Governor proceeded to water down further. By the time it was finished and submitted is was not worth the paper it was written on.

The end result was, I went before the multi-agency steering committee, with useless vision in hand and proceeded to redraft the vision verbally until I had unanimous (unbelievable for government) approval on the final vision statement that, low and behold, was vastly similar to what I started with. The problem had been one we have spoken of earlier, the level of trust. I had previously little face-to-face time with either the Chief of Staff or the Governor so I had to wait until such an opportunity could present itself that I could meet everyone involved and "sell" the vision. It was the personal delivery of the speech and my commitment to the vision (and some substantial leg work to achieve preliminary allies) that allowed me to penetrate the hidden agendas and gain the trust necessary for execution of the vision statement. The crafting and approval process for the vision statement provided yet another excellent example to reinforce how Tacit knowledge must be brokered face-to-face to achieve results.

With this in mind let's look at a sample Vision statement:

> *It is the goal of this organization to cultivate an environment in which its people are constantly striving for gains in both performance and innovation. What we" know" makes a significant contribution to the value of our enterprise and our stakeholders. The sharing of our knowledge only furthers our efforts in adding value and commitment to our mission and financial objectives.*
>
> *Knowledge should be an enabler of both performance and innovation, should better empower our people to undertake their daily tasks and provide an avenue of growth in every area or our organization.*
>
> *Our vision is to create the infrastructure necessary to facilitate the sharing of knowledge throughout the enterprise. This infrastructure will support the management of existing knowledge, the teaching and mentoring of our human resources, the reduction of redundancy and provide mechanisms to aid in person-to-person communications.*
>
> *To this end it is our goal to utilize processes, methodologies, programs and technologies to deliver the necessary components that will engage the people of this organization, as well as others that participate outside our organization, in a long-term knowledge transfer strategy. In essence, our objectives are to capture into our human resource programs and technological systems both existing knowledge as well as providing the vehicles for knowledge exchange.*

From a technological perspective infrastructure must be comprised of and support systems that can pull-in, push-out, index, categorize and analyze our existing knowledge. The same technology infrastructure should also facilitate face-to-face communications, provide systems that enable users to locate and qualify potential repositories of knowledge (both human and technological) and provide recognition to participants for their value-added efforts.

Participation from our staff, our partners and our customers is paramount to success. All departments, divisions, sections and agencies must undertake to develop programs that both recognize and reward the efforts of our participants and encourage their on-going participation, nurturing their desire to transfer their knowledge to others and strive for ever-increasing quality in the their personal knowledge gaining efforts.

Perhaps not Shakespeare, but the intent of the Vision is clear. The terminology is focused but generic enough to leave room for innovation on human resource and technological sides. A long-term vision should not emphasize specific products, programs or technologies because of the fluid nature of each. We strive not to back ourselves into corners in anything but to articulate and maintain a 50,000-foot perspective and direction.

CHAPTER 4—
Knowledge Roles and Titles

As far as I'm concerned Roles are far more important than Titles.
Roles wrap parameters around our expectations of a knowledge
worker. Roles provide a vehicle for us to define metrics that allow us
to measure knowledge worker deliverables. Titles only provide social
statements and since everyone is a Vice-President these days the statements are pretty weak.

I came across a humorous parody on titles during my research so I
thought I would include it.

Ethan Winning is a nationally known author, is president of E.A.
Winning associates, Inc., a Walnut Creek, California employee rela-
tions consulting firm specializing in tailoring employee handbooks
and performance and compensation systems. He is also the author of
"Labor Pains: Employer and Employee Rights and Obligations" (3rd
edition, Sept. 1997).

In a recent conversation I had with Ethan he also informed me that he
had just run across his very first "Chief People Officer". After reading
his article you will see why his candor on the subject diminished his
chances of a long-term relationship with the newly appointed CPO at
the moment of introduction.

Here is part of his article:

THE CHIEF KNOWLEDGE OFFICER

Much as my techno-clients dislike the thought of a hierarchy, it became apparent that not only would the information age spawn a new hierarchy, it would be ameboid in shape and incomprehensible to anyone on the outside looking in. I decided not to be left behind this time, and took off to interview an old friend of mine who just happened to be the new chief knowledge officer for GIGO Corp.

As I entered GIGO, the first thing I noticed was that it had been cubicalized, sort of a 1990's version of a 1960s IBM. However, in order to make up for the cell-like division of status, there was a foosball game in the middle of the reception area, and the dress code seemed to have been "downsized" to Birkenstocks and shorts. As one GIGO employee explained, "Levis are okay, too, if not a bit stuffy, but you know, it's hot out and all that stuff." "If that's stuffy, what do you consider formal," I asked? "Oh, that would be a t-shirt with no writing on it," he replied.

Josh Joshonson ("PH" to his friends) is the 28-year old president of GIGO. I'd known him since college back in the 50's. He greeted me warmly and showed me into his office. At first I thought that his walls were tiled but upon close inspection found that they were made up of AOL and CompuServe trial subscription disks. Other than that his office was reminiscent of a college dorm room, and one had the distinct feeling that the mess was planned.

EW: "Josh, I think it's great that you've been made president of GIGO."

Josh: "No, I'm the CKO, Chief Knowledge Officer. We don't have a president, per se. We did away with the title after old whatshisname was squeezed out."

EW: "I noticed that there was a little politicking going on down here. How'd you do it?"

Josh: "I didn't have to do anything. It was well known that I had the most knowledge, so I became the CKO. Besides, I'm the only member of MENSA so it was almost a foregone conclusion. Kind of like Ronn Owens, only smarter and with two web sites."

EW: "So if you're the smartest, you get to be pres...uh... CKO?"

Josh: "No, you don't have to be the smartest. You have to have the most knowledge."

EW: "That's strange. You can know a lot without having any ideas."

Josh: "Ideas? Oh, for that you'd want to talk with our Chief Concept Officer. I don't think you quite understand the structure. Here, let me show you...". Josh brought out an organization chart, renamed a "Corporate Conceptualization Pyramid." It looked something like this....

CHIEF KNOWLEDGE OFFICER
    Chief Concept Officer
        Chief Thought Officer
            Chief Opinion Officer
                Chief Information Officer

EW: "I don't get it. First of all, I'd think that the chief information officer would be just under you."

Josh: "Uh, uh. The CIO is the disseminator of information, and he can't disseminate anything until it's been thought up. After someone thinks of something, usually our Idea Officer, it's passed on to the T&O Departments, then to me, and then we tell the world about it."

EW: "T&O?"

Josh: "Sorry. Thought and Opinion."

EW: "Well, the concept of knowledge workers called for teams. Where are the...pardon the expression...rank and file?"

Josh: "I'll humor you on that one. Okay, other than a secretary who has the title of 'Word Fabrication Artist,' there's no one under the Chief Concept Officer. But under the Chief Thought Officer we do have the core of our employee-contributors: There are Thinkers, Reflectors, Cogitators, and Deliberators, all with senior and junior titles depending on their SAT scores...if they had to go to college...

[It was then that I noticed the framed, unsigned, limited edition photograph of Bill Gates on the wall. My mind wandered. I wondered if it was coming back, but then I heard...]
"...When an idea has been thought, reflected upon, cogitated and deliberated, it's passed downward for an opinion. This is an important step because the Opinion Department has the Senior Believers, the Judgment Officers, and those with Real Convictions. Below them are the Assumption Clerks and Notion Aides. Once an idea is believed, it

goes to our Dogma Department which is directly under the Chief Information Officer although, truth be told, it really doesn't become dogma until I say it's dogma."

EW: "Seems to me that some pretty good ideas could get lost in the process."

Josh: "Find a few, lose a few."

EW: "And this one made it all the way to the top of GIGO?"

Josh: "Hey, you can't argue with success. Did you see that our stock has doubled this year to 6? If this keeps up we were thinking of an IPO starting at somewhere around 140. Hey, did you see the picture of my new yacht in the paper the other day. It's a beaut and cost a bundle!"

EW: "No such thing as a free launch, huh? How do you make money around here?"

Josh: "Well, most of it comes from our Cyber Vocabulary Department, you know, the one that sells new words to Internet advertisers."

EW: "Words like?"

Josh: "Like 'cyberad,' 'electromedia,' or 'digital insertion device'…although that one did come out of our Acronym Department."

EW: "And there are people who actually pay for that? You must have done a hell of a job of marketing. What happens when an idea bombs?"

Josh: "Every once in a while we do have one of those, but it never makes it out of the building. The reason we've been so successful is because of these three departments [pointing to the bottom of the chart], Collaboration, Corroboration, Alibi. Hey, I'm headed down there right now. Then I've got to stop by Creative Numbers Crunching. We've got some of those PBS elves in today.. Want to come along?"

EW: [Don't ask…] "No thanks, I think I'll just go home and read the paper. How do I get out of here?"

Josh: "Just go past Foundations, through Notions, and take a right."

Additional information on Ethan can be found at his web site at: http://www.ewin.com.

Defining Knowledge Roles and Responsibilities

We need to clearly articulate each knowledge workers specific roles and responsibilities. I also feel that each knowledge worker should participate in the creation of these roles and responsibilities as they are also supposed to be the experts in their given area. Mutual development of the roles and responsibilities also enable the knowledge worker to identify areas in which they may experience obstacles to delivery and allow management and the knowledge worker to re-engineer their requirements to eliminate these obstacles. All roles and responsibilities should also be reviewed at least annually to determine inefficiencies in the descriptions.

For my example I will create the role and responsibilities for an Information Security Officer.

Sample Role and Responsibilities:

Scope
This policy establishes the minimum administrative responsibilities for the agency appointed Information Security Officer (ISO). The IT Section is responsible for the security of all Agency data information resources. IT Section specific procedures developed to conform with other Agency policies must be reviewed frequently to reflect changes in personnel and technology."

Community
Intended Audience—This document is intended for Agency
                     Management Staff

Benefactors—The beneficiaries of this document will be Agency Staff

Document Owner—Document owner Dr. Randy Frid

Information Security Administration Functions
Each Division and Section must formally delegate responsibility and authority for all information security matters. Many individuals across organizational lines may be involved as long as there is a clear separation of duties and responsibilities which provides effective checks, balances and accountability. However, it is important that one individual be designated as having primary responsibility for coordination of agency information security. It is also important that another individual be designated as a back-up ISO.

Role of an Information Security Officer
An ISO's duty is to ensure that information security policies and procedures are established and implemented to protect the information assets of the Agency, participate in the creation and review of the poli-

cies and procedures, recommend security strategies, and keep information security systems current. The agency must have procedures to
prevent, detect, contain and recover from information security
breaches from both internal and external sources and disasters both
natural and man made. The ISO has a duty to ensure that these procedures are in place.

In order to develop successful information security, the ISO:
- needs to strike a balance between security and the agency's
  mission by assessing risk and determining organizational needs;
- needs to understand the agency's mission, how each information system supports that mission, how they are intercon-
  nected, and the associated technology;
- needs a stable resource base in terms of personnel, funds, and
  other support in order to plan and execute security programs
  and projects effectively;
- needs agency wide cooperation to successfully implement
  information security;
- needs to coordinate and call upon others in the agency for
  assistance; and
- needs to establish links to security personnel in other parts of
  the organization, to other ISOs in other agencies, and to
  external security sources.

Recommended: Establish an advisory board of employees who represent different functions/disciplines across the organization to help
develop policies and procedures and maintain continuity for information security across the organization on an ongoing basis.

The ISO's role is to:
- report to the IT Manager, to balance security with technological and programmatic issues;
- be the agency's authority on information security;

- recommend appropriate separation of duties and responsibilities for (IT) functions;
- promote information security awareness throughout the agency;
- be part of the decision-making team when the agency is *designing, planning, procuring* or *upgrading* technologies;
- be responsible for the development, implementation and revisions of an agency information security policy;
- be the single point of contact for all issues involving information security including, but not limited to, questions, alerts, viruses and breaches; and
- inform the IT Manager of breaches, information security activity and risks.

Training/Education

All employees, agents and others who access agency computer systems must be provided with sufficient training and supporting reference materials to allow them to properly protect agency information.

Training is an integral aspect of information security and will contribute to a secure computing environment. This training must encompass all users, including executive management, program, field, IT and other staff. Trained users will be able to be proactive in assisting to ensure there is a secure environment and to recognize if and when a breach occurs.

The ISO should also keep current on all areas of information security including but not limited to alerts, warnings, viruses, and new techniques. Therefore, the ISO should receive information security and appropriate technical training on a regular basis. Certification may be pursued if the agency deems it necessary. This may be a worthwhile way to ensure the ISO is familiar with all areas of information security. Certification of an ISO is highly recommended.

The ISO's role is to:
- identify appropriate training for agency staff including, but not limited to, the information security policy;
- be familiar with and understand all access security methods and configurations at the agency;
- stay current via training and publications about information security issues;
- review and test information security features of new critical software, hardware and firmware;
- promote the education of agency staff about the information security risks, including social engineering and the presence of unauthorized persons;
- receive regular training on information security issues; and
- review publications and other information regarding information security.

Agency Information Security Policy

A key portion of the ISO's role is to develop and implement an agency-specific information security policy in concert with the appropriate staff. The staff should include, but not be limited to, IT managers, IT personnel, program staff, legal, human resources, program managers and executive management. The ISO must work with the appropriate groups to develop and periodically review the agency's information security policy and guidelines.

System and Network Access

Each Division/section shall have an information security policy that defines access and requires notification of the ISO of changes in the status of users. All requests for access and changes in user status must be processed through the ISO. The ISO should compare the request with the security policy, and if in compliance with the information security policy, forward the request to the appropriate group for access implementation. The ISO should receive confirmation of access authorizations, keeping a log of who has access and the level of access.

Monitoring Activity

Monitoring includes day-to-day and investigative activities. Daily monitoring allows the agency to proactively detect patterns of usage that can pinpoint anomalies, which may trigger the need for investigation. Monitoring activities include review of intrusion detection reports as well as review of daily usage logs. Such monitoring shall include: servers, mainframes, firewalls, networks and applications. Monitoring logs must be available to the ISO at any time.

Incidents/Investigations

The agency's information security policy must include procedures for reporting the description of the information security incident, the type of incident, how it is reported and to whom. For example, an incident may be the report of a virus on a computer, denial of services, a security breach, any sign of intrusion or theft of information.

The ISO's role is to:
- ensure that the information security policy reflects current security practices and architecture;
- take appropriate steps in accordance with the agency's information security policy when breaches occur, which may include:
- being notified immediately when an incident occurs;
- immediately ascertaining the scope, nature and extent of the breach;
- notifying the appropriate executive management of the incident;
- isolating and containing the incident;
- preserving evidence where appropriate; and
- taking steps to prevent a reoccurrence of the incident.

Preparing for Contingencies and Disasters

The agency's information security policy must include a plan of action in the event of a natural or man-made disaster occurring. The ISO will lead contingency planning effort. The contingency plans must address how to keep secure the agency's critical functions operating in the event of disruptions, both large and small.

Risk Analysis

Information security risk analysis is a process used to determine an agency's vulnerabilities in information security versus its required level of security.

The ISO should assist staff in assessing information security risks. The risk analysis provides the manager with informed choices about cost, vulnerabilities and solutions.

Hardware and Software Inventory

The information security policy must require a current inventory of all hardware, software and license compliance. Such inventory must be reviewed minimally on an annual basis to assure compliance with the information security policy and the license agreements.

Summary of ISO Role and Responsibilities

It is the responsibility of the IT Manager to appoint an ISO. This person must be well versed in all areas of information security and be able to understand the technology being used at the Agency. Each piece of information security must fit together and a strong ISO will act as the cornerstone of the agency's information security structure.

CHAPTER 5—
Identifying and Categorizing Your Knowledge

In this phase of building a knowledge management system we need to look at the type of data, information and knowledge we want to capture and transfer. We spoke earlier that if we captured all the data, information and knowledge we have into a central system, then the resultant return on a search would likely present us with so many variables that we would mentally weigh the amount of time it would take to sort through the pile of information and decide quite quickly that the return on effort is not worth the time.

Therefore we need to decide in advance how we want to structure or classify our knowledge so that we can perform preliminary filtering and present the most relevant information in the shortest possible time and in a format that makes the review of such data, information and knowledge clearly legible and intuitive.

The first step in sorting information is to review the departmental design of the organization as a good starting point for determining the logical structure of knowledge. This isn't always going to be correct but most companies organize their business units the way they think and work together. For instance, the sales department of an organization may span the globe but the sales employees usually share a common vision dictated by the business plan. They also share experiences, customers, products and processes. The sales department, in turn, may also want pipeline information from engineering, marketing, service, accounting and human resources. Collectively, they may want to begin to see relationships, trends, patterns and information from these areas to provide higher levels in accuracy for their own forecasting.

Now we need to identify the data stores that hold the relevant data, information and knowledge. These were found in step 11 of your research map. Once the stores are identified we move on to building the crucial site vocabulary.

The site vocabulary is commonly a set of nouns that can be used throughout the enterprise to identify pieces of knowledge and relate them to other pieces of knowledge. It starts best to create a set of high-level nouns that can be used in broad generalized classification.

First-level category words typically reflect the top-level departmental-ization used throughout the enterprise: Sales, Marketing, Research, Accounting, etc...

Second-level category words will begin to break down the depart-ments into subcategories such as Sales being broken down into: Continents, Countries, Regions, Cities, etc... There is no limit on the size of vocabulary but building a large and complex vocabulary often presents the users with too many association choices when saving data and they begin to look for shortcuts.

You can also build other vocabularies that will address specific aspects of your organization.

This vocabulary will become critical **"Meta Data"** tags that can be used to search, sort and index data, information and knowledge. Meta Data tags are bound to pieces of knowledge but stored separately from, or are imbedded in, the content. These Meta Data tags can then be indexed and sorted according to the requirements of the individual user. Meta Data tags must be consistent across the enterprise to maintain the integrity of the search.

As you can tell, this is not all that complicated but the nouns decided in this stage must be formalized and utilized across the entire enterprise. Achieving utilization and enforcement of these nouns can be done through both technology and policy.

Policy enforcement is always used so that consistency is maintained throughout the organization. You don't want one department going off building a vocabulary that doesn't bind to the rest of the organizational vocabulary or the ability to consolidate data during searches becomes weakened. For example, if one user stores a piece of knowledge and is able to type in "Wyoming" as the state while another user enters "WY" as the state then a search for all information about Wyoming will only return one of the two entries.

There are different technological methods for binding this vocabulary of Meta data to pieces of data, information and knowledge. One method would be the use of a product such as Microsoft Site Server that offers a web-based knowledge manager component. Other technologies that can participate in enterprise-wide vocabularies are Directory Services such as LDAP that can be used by many systems including Microsoft Site Server. Desktop applications, such as those bundled in Microsoft Office allow users to enter Meta Data information into the properties section of a document or spreadsheet when saving. For more information on Microsoft Site Server, Microsoft Office 2000 and LDAP see Chapter 8.

Regardless of the delivery mechanism, we always need to categorize the knowledge we intend on collecting. Once we have categorized the information, then we can decide who needs it most often so we can physically locate the data closest to the end users. Having the knowledge we need close-by usually means we receive faster information. Fast is good because people rarely enjoy waiting for information. As we spoke of early, people will tend to lean towards faster information more than accurate information. Therefore, carefully filtered and categorized information, located close to the users will typically produce favorable results in usability.

The inception of a Knowledge Management System (KMS) will typically begin with the "brain dump" of initial data and information into a central repository. This works well as a testing ground for an Explicit KMS. A central repository at least captures some the information we want and provides a vehicle to search and retrieve the information required to help in decision-making. Without the inclusion of Meta Data our ability to categorize and physically relocate our knowledge is seriously impaired. Therefore, the development of an enterprise vocabulary and the enforcement of Meta Data, through technology and policy, is a crucial step in the development of a knowledge management system.

CHAPTER 6—
The Cultural Infrastructure Components

Overview

Culture is the heart and sole of knowledge management. There has never been a project that I have worked on that did not require cultural re-engineering to be successful. A case in point, I'm currently working on a project (which will remain nameless to protect the innocent) where, after first walking through the door I could sense during our first meeting the internal turmoil, political jockeying and social stagnation. The words "job security" were permanently tattooed on everyone's tongues and thus tainted everything they have to say as the words rolled off their tongues to escape their lips. Even their body language and the location where they would sit spoke of isolation and insecurity.

Two associates joined me in the first days of engagement and after the first day we agreed amongst ourselves that the only deliverable we could hope for in this first phase is to build up a level of trust, at the most, in our technical abilities and hopefully our consulting company. As it turns out, during our discovery research, the CIO was new to the organization and many internal staff had positioned for her job and lost to an outsider. Many of the senior staff were upset and rebelled in subtle but malicious ways. We are talking about many long-term employees with the sole goal of retirement in their vision scope. They didn't want anyone rocking their perfect little isolated worlds and making them accountable for their actions.

We were there to begin researching and modeling a major technology renovation that would upset every aspect of their daily jobs and force everyone to learn new technologies, processes and methodologies. They thought they had the world of technology in their back pockets until we stepped on site. The new CIO had been living in the real world and knew that this organization must undertake a significant re-engineering effort if it was, in any way, to be able to deliver the technology solutions the enterprise was demanding. A mandate from the top had decided to integrate many of the current functions throughout the enterprise in an effort to reduce redundancy, increase communications and provide a new smoother solution-set for its clients.

I discovered early on that there was no documentation on anything, individuals in the IT section kept their respective jewels of knowledge exclusively to themselves and cultivated the concept of "he who knows the most and keeps it completely to themselves lives the longest". I knew that there were fundamental problems in both culture and technology and began developing a knowledge management strategy to set the wrongs right.

Fortunately the CIO had mastered one of the principle concepts of knowledge management: You don't need to know everything, you just have to know where to go to find it. She called in Omni Technology Centers from Atlanta and had us come out and perform a first phase assessment of the situation to provide third party validation of her concerns. Our assessment aligned with hers and provided the technical evidence to support her claims. This gave her a clear understanding of what was wrong, but more importantly it told her why. Now the question became one of what to do about it.

I first needed to repair the culture so that the IT members would begin transferring their proprietary knowledge to the rest of the IT Section staff. They needed to document what they knew and capture the knowledge to a repository that could be accessed by all. I needed to formalize the mundane daily processes so that others could also participate without having to re-invent the wheel every time. I then needed to get the repetitive tasks into the hands of the juniors and get the senior staff to spend more time in team discussions, collaboration and providing insight into the business problems at hand and drive them to delivering innovative solutions.

Something completely foreign to this organization was the concept of "team building". Employees worked as isolated islands and cultivated their privacy. This is not an atypical problem as our culture tends to worship the sole superstar when we think of the Bill Gates and Albert Einstein's of the world. Unfortunately, our literature and representation of these individuals often fails to account for or emphasize the value of the tens, hundreds and often thousands of people that participate diligently in delivering the support these individuals require. A classic example is the Michelangelo masterpiece, the ceiling of the Sistine Chapel. In our mind's eye, we see Michelangelo, looking remarkably like Charlton Heston, laboring alone on the scaffolding high above the chapel floor. In fact, 13 people helped paint the work. Michelangelo was not only an artist; he was, as biographer William E. Wallace points out, the head of a good-sized entrepreneurial enterprise.

I set about redesigning the reporting structure. As step one, I eliminated all titles and formal reporting mechanisms in the IT section. Everyone now reported to me temporarily. Following the elimination of titles, communications broke down. This was a good thing as tempers began to flare and people began to drop their private world facades and expose their desires, frustrations and skills. It became evident quite quickly who the team leaders were, who could negotiate and who could articulate themselves. As problems rose, those with the skills to solve the problems quickly became apparent and we had a chance to measure their skills against real world problems and pick suitable teams for them to work in.

I quickly came to realize that many of the staff were in positions they should have never been in. Many in management positions had little or no management capability, and worse, they did not have the respect of their workers. As a matter of fact, the lack of respect and trust was pervasive.

I broke the IT department into six logical groupings: Programming, Database, Web, Networking, Security and Help Desk. I designed six officer roles (not titles) and proceeded to take the employees that seemed the obvious team leaders, the most motivated to communicate and learn, and assigned them each a specific role. These people formed the first team. The officers had the responsibility of generating and advertising standards and policy for their respective roles. They were forced to meet each morning to recap their efforts and each member of this team had to account fully for their hours and efforts. Each of the other team members had the opportunity to question the viability of the others efforts and time expenditures as it was made clear that if one team member failed they all failed and would be held accountable.

Within a couple of weeks this team was talking, fighting, debating, analyzing and solving problems that had plagued the organization for years. I facilitated the meetings and demanded everything to be documented and posted so all IT staff could review and respond. Capturing the thought process was paramount on my agenda. It's a waste of valuable knowledge transfer to just make decisions and present the resultant; the rationale behind the decision is really the most crucial piece. Allowing others to review, digest, and comment on the thought process forces us to test our knowledge at every step. If it cannot withstand the tests than the knowledge isn't knowledge, its just dogma and should be supplanted by true, validated knowledge. Many of the team members were internally nervous about having their knowledge put to the test and they all were humbled when they found out their knowledge was limited and weak in areas they had beforehand considered and advertised themselves as experts. But during the humbling process, they soon began to realize that they were all being humbled in one aspect or another and nobody was really an island of crucifixion.

It took those first few brave soles to face the knowledge testing firing squad before they all came to understand that they could survive and grow from the experience. They began to let down their hair and publicly expose their weaknesses and strengths. They had begun the slow process of learning to trust each other and to trust in the knowledge of their team members. They were no longer afraid to put someone else's knowledge to the test and make them stand up and prove their knowledge using supporting evidence and logic. They each contributed to the growing knowledge pool and forced each other to document the thoughts and rationale for the others to see and query. The energy level shifted upwards in order of magnitude and a new sense of self worth began to cultivate in each of the team and in the team as a whole. Just watching the discussion threads that came from the meetings was exciting for everyone else as they could see the level of knowledge transfer and the sheer quality of the discussions continued to escalate with each meeting. The deliverables from the meetings became concise, focused, well documented and most of all innovative. The cool thing about Tiggers is that they bounce. The same can be said for the human spirit.

At this point the team began to welcome other members because they could offer new insights, additional testing, expand the value-base of the entire knowledge team and provide even greater innovation. It is interesting to see that new team members were initially distrusted until they past the humbling stage and exposed their strengths and especially their weaknesses. Once the team could understand a new team member's limitations then there was a psychological barrier that had been broached and trust had been established. Order would return and creative conflict would once again rise and stimulate creative thinking.

After the initial success I broke up the first team into additional teams and absorbed more of the IT population into the other teams so the original team could begin disseminating what they had learned about team building. It was obvious that, because they had never worked in teams, that they had no project management framework. So I began to train the initial team on a simple project management framework using the Trinity (scope, timeline and budget). I taught them the value of assessing their daily functions as projects and how to build a business case around their projects. I taught them how to assess financial impact and to bind their very existence in the organization back to the departmental funding model. I taught them the usage and value of Risk, Issue, Opportunity and Change management techniques and how to proxy decisions.

I then had the team leaders meet with the department heads throughout the organization to determine what their customers Critical Success Factors were and how to use the CSF's as the framework for building their business cases and assessing the value of building and maintaining the technologies to support the CSF's. I finally taught them the basics of corporate accounting so they could financially rationalize their department, processes, technologies and staffing requirements. In other words I lead the transfer of knowledge by example so they could get a true sense of the value of knowledge sharing.

With this newfound knowledge the teams began to question and define everything they could analyze. They documented their thoughts and held open debate forums. I challenged them and they challenged me. The support systems came under question at every turn and the existence of existing systems and processes succumbed to innovation and logic. The CIO was ecstatic about the results and could begin spending her time on enterprise-level objective setting and politics. She in turn captured her thought process and used the exact same tools and techniques for communicating her ideas. Teams began to challenge her decisions and innovation on all sides blossomed.

The ending of this anecdote is that we still had deep-rooted HR problems, but then again knowledge management does not encompass all the functions of HR. Knowledge management is a framework for the collection, dissemination and brokering of knowledge. We planted the seeds for a new attitude and new practices and it has begun to digest the rest of the organization and the CIO is spearheading the knowledge management efforts throughout.

Team Size

Let's start at the top. There are three classifications of organizational structure: The Team, The Department and The Organization.

The Team is found throughout society. A team will consist of two to six members and will be bound by a loose association that targets a specific task or function. As I spoke of earlier, team members are hunter-gatherers and come together to perform a specific task or function then disband. Teams are usually formed quickly and causally and have no formal structure. No one is typically the "boss" although there is usually someone on the team that emerges as an untitled leader and guides the decision making process as the work progresses. Within a team the unspoken role of team leader will often pass from one person to another depending on what function is being performed at that moment, dictated by the individual skill-sets required at that time. Teams are typically a democracy and everyone has a voice. Team interactions are usually passionate and intense as each team member relies on the others for a successful outcome, and success and failure to achieve the end result is obvious and immediate.

The Department usually consists of several teams. Studies have shown that departments are best kept to six teams or less. Departments often have a "boss" but the boss will usually proclaim that his or her group is really a democracy to avoid any contention that he or she is the dominant authority. Regardless of declared democracy, someone in the department, whether it's the formally designated boss or not, will assume a leadership role to facilitate decision-making. This leader usually rises to the top because of other departmental members respect for their knowledge or organizational skills. Whoever takes the leader-ship role will not typically lead by enforcing a dominant position, instead he or she will lead by example and attempt to achieve consen-sus amongst the departmental members. Departmental members are also usually well informed of everything that is going on and may offer input as they wish. There are strong personal feelings of each departmental member to achieve the department's objectives as a whole and to work as a synchronized unit. If a department grows to more than six teams then it usually destabilizes and fractionalizes into two separate departments. Too large a social and political structure cannot be maintained through consensus.

The Organization is a formal political mechanism to manage multiple departments. It does not operate on the same basis as Teams or Departments. There must be a formal line of authority as it is almost impossible to get everyone to agree on every issue. Therefore someone or some group of people need to make decisions that will not please everyone all the time. Those that are displeased with decisions that have been made must conform to the top-level vote or leave the organization. The formal hierarchy also produces the necessary infrastructure for communications with other organizations. The organization provides the politics and bureaucracy for formal exchange outside the organization.

Size Counts

Team Size counts. Throughout the years I have worked on teams of various sizes, some more effective than others. The larger teams always seemed less productive and much more difficult to control than smaller teams. I started to muse that there must be some rationale that could be found that would tell me what the optimum team size should be and why.

During my research efforts I stumbled upon a book written by Collin Renfrew called "Theory and Explanation of Archaeology" that talks in depth about organizational structure and scalar stress. I can summarize the relevant sections quickly by stating, *"The ability to make decisions degrades rapidly as the team size grows beyond six."* Many studies have been made on the limitations of the human mind to determine capacities and limitations. The end result is that it appears the human mind only has the ability to handle up to seven concurrent functions simultaneously. One such study by AT&T drew the same conclusions and became the basis for the eventual adoption of the seven-digit telephone number, with the rationale that the human mind could store and recall up to seven digits as a single unit of work. Additional numbers became more difficult to manage, as they didn't fit into the single memory chunks and needed to utilize two separate memory actions to recall the entire number.

After my research I looked back over time at my own experiences and found the similarities in previous teams I've worked on. Perhaps not the most objective review, but the results seemed very similar to my research findings. When working on a team of six or less people we always assumed a team approach with all of us carrying the same levels of responsibility and authority (no matter what the business card titles read). If another team member was added, someone almost always evolved subconsciously to become the team lead and we would always filter our project reporting back though this individual. We didn't always formally declare a leader but someone would always assume this responsibility and we would all subliminally acknowledge the role. If we added more than six members to the team I could begin sensing the political edge that would begin shortly after the new member had acclimatized. The atmosphere would begin to tense in formal meetings and if the team had grown to eight members then the even number made it difficult to break a tie when decisions were split. It became easier to break the project into two working teams that would report to a formal project manager. So in essence we demanded the nomination of a leader just to offload the politics that had begun to grow.

Nowadays I build all my teams with six or less people. Then I set out to prove that I am worthy of being a team member through demonstration of personal knowledge, compassion and vision. I work very hard to initially establish my credibility with the team because I find people put little stake in titles when working in a team environment. Team leaders will usually surface early because of the level of trust they gain by example.

Training/Mentoring Programs

With the multitude of human resource training guides and HR companies on the market today there is little need for me to attempt to invent the utopian training/mentoring program for a company. Simply put, there is no Utopia for training/mentoring. Any and all methodologies carry some merit so long as they drive at the transfer of knowledge throughout the enterprise.

Technology can be capitalized upon as a vehicle to deliver the crucial information we need to help make decisions, but the knowledge we use to finalize a decision is forever trapped in the minds of the people. Do not look on technology as your knowledge management resource, use technology to establish communication mechanisms to connect the right people at the right time and serve them the information they need as a team to provide supporting evidence and a framework for innovation.

Programs that are of value that I have used personally include such things as:

Case Studies

Analyzing particular projects, sub-projects and tasks at weekly meetings are excellent methods of reviewing strategy, processes, lessons learned (especially mistakes made). As someone once wrote "learn from other peoples mistakes, you simply don't have enough time to make them all yourself". Then document your discussions and findings. Capture all results into your knowledge base. Opportunities are also of extreme importance to capture during these studies. Even small opportunities can be used to better your processes.

Focus Groups

Collect a group of people (customers, managers, staff) together to debate the merits of someone's idea. You be surprised at what you learn in most cases. We make a lot of presumptions during the daily course of our jobs and all too often frequently miss the nature of the beast altogether. Then document your discussions and findings. Capture all results into your knowledge base.

Feedback Systems

Send out questionnaires (electronic, paper, it doesn't matter) to get the feedback from those affected by your work. This can go to anyone, internal or external that can offer potential insight into areas you may not even have thought of let alone areas you are weak in your judgment on. Then document your discussions and findings. Capture all results into your knowledge base.

Performance Evaluations

Tell them how they are doing. Measure them against some known metrics. Be brutally honest, a sugarcoated evaluation does no one any good. This should not be relegated to managers either. This should really be in the hands of the team itself. Appraise each other; assess how well each is communicating with the others. Then document your discussions and findings. Capture all results into your knowledge base.

If a team member doesn't fit, escalate it to management and management must either relocate the team member or remove them all together. Yes, it's a hard decision to make, but not making the decision is a lot worse for the team as well as the organization.

Knowledge Seminars

Periodically hold seminars in your own offices and allow the teams to demonstrate what they are doing, even if only in conversational format. Make the other teams aware of other projects and other resources of knowledge in their enterprise. Then document your discussions and findings. Capture all results into your knowledge base.

Bring in outsiders on a regular basis to talk about what they are doing in their particular fields of expertise. We can get far too buried in our daily routine to notice the world is passing us by. We have to avoid continuous inbreeding if we are expected to grow, succeed and assimilate into the world around us.

Broadcast Communications

Newsletters, divisional or enterprise e-mail notices, fly-ers… It doesn't really matter what vehicle works, it's the message of recognition for some and the lessons learned from failures from others. Don't ever disguise or bury failures as no one can benefit from the experience otherwise. Propaganda that is only positive begins to sound like marketing material and is quickly discounted as untrustworthy. This information should be reported like a newspaper documenting a story with corroborating evidence and thought stimulating commentary. Copy all communications into your knowledge base.

Rewards for Achievement

Design a good reward program for innovation and contributions and participation in enterprise knowledge. This could be a simple as recognition or as complicated as promotion or monetary gains. Once again, it is the intent, not the delivery.

Contractors and Consultants

In the ever-increasing world of knowledge workers there is a growing demand for specialists in the form of contractors and consultants. It is no longer practical to maintain staff positions for every area of expertise you'll need as you build your organization. Most staff positions are fundamentally operational in nature and the time allocated to these workers often leaves little time for learning new processes, techniques or technologies. Implementing change in the enterprise will more often than not, require the assistance of those that are well experienced and have special skills in the area of change that you are heading.

The problem posed for management is one of creating an internal culture that considers contractors and consultants part of the business norm. Too often I have seen staff, which have not been prepared for the inclusion of contractors and consultants, become territorial and feel threatened. Management that has not prepared their staff for the world of contractors and consultants will need to deal with increasing levels of conflict and decreasing levels of morale in staff members.

We need to cultivate in our staff the perception that contractors and consultants serve a valuable purpose. When we bring in contractors and consultants our primary intention is knowledge transfer. As I've stated elsewhere, it not only provides us the opportunity to achieve our end results with greater accuracy and a higher level of confidence, it also brings us face-to-face with new and innovative ideas and practices. Using contractors and consultants also helps us avoid inbreeding, which can create pockets of lethargy and complacency.

Contractors and Consultants bring great advantage to organizations and we need to educate our staff to these advantages so they can partake in the knowledge transfer and maximize the investment made in external knowledge resources.

Virtual Teams

Teams can reside anywhere provided you follow a basic premise that team members require face-to-face communications to be effective. Technologically they need to have the right infrastructure to deliver this level of communication.

I have spoken in detail of the benefits of teams but in today's world these teams can span the globe. We need to cultivate the benefits of teams throughout an enterprise if we hope to nurture our knowledge transfer efforts. We need to assess the amount of available bandwidth for each team member's participation into a virtual team environment. In order to facilitate face-to-face communications we need to determine what types of technologies we can use to deliver the end result.

We can use technological tools such as stand-alone analog or digital video conferencing systems or network video conferencing and application collaboration tools such as Microsoft's NetMeeting tool. Each system has its pros and cons. Dedicated video conferencing devices are more expensive, usually requiring greater bandwidth than their desktop counterparts and are typically used in joining meeting rooms together for shared team meetings. These systems usually provide better resolution of images providing a more definitive look and feel for the participants.

The desktop video conferencing packages, such as NetMeeting require the deployment of individual digital cameras and sound systems to the desktops of each participant as well as the deployment of an ILS (Internet Locator Server) which will provide the necessary directory for locating and connecting to participants. The benefit of a desktop video conferencing system is that it provides greater spontaneity of meetings, no requirement to schedule meeting rooms, and allows for additional on-line collaboration such as shared white boarding and shared applications. The size of screen and resolution is limited by bandwidth availability but these systems can typically run as low as 28.8Kb/s, which is a lowest common denominator for telephone connectivity these days. Any greater availability of bandwidth only enhances quality of picture and refresh rates of graphics.

Formal and Informal meetings

As I documented in my above experience of team building in the current organization, so it applies to every other undertaking I've participated in. The face-to-face meetings broke all old testaments of power and isolation. It is not only recommended, but I believe to be imperative that teams hold both formal and informal meetings. Formal meetings can be leveraged to test the continuity and rationalization of a team, project or ideas. Informal meetings are better for teams to hold without management to discuss negligence of particular team members to carry their weight. The informal peer review is all-powerful in corporate troubleshooting. It protects everyone from the experience of formal management reprimands that nobody likes.

Formal meetings are best suited to a weekly schedule to avoid information overload and protect against complacency. Meeting start times are rigid and should be held to sternly. Time is money and nobody likes to kick off meetings to have someone walk in late and need to be briefed on "where we're at".

Informal meetings can be so powerful that many Japanese corporations have established tearooms and enforce team staff to take a mandatory tea break for 30-60 minutes every day. This concept replaces the old "water cooler" break that is so often lost in corporate re-engineering efforts. In the past, as people gathered in small groups around the water cooler they would almost invariably talk about organizational ills. They rarely talk about the good things and rarely talk about the weather. These informal gatherings have been the conduit to many innovative ideas or at least the exposure of symptomatic problems in the enterprise. North Americans typically take the attitude that this time is unproductive, and management, for the most part, want the employees to go back to their cubicles and get back to "real" work. This attitude has helped destroy much creativity in today's flattened organizations.

Capturing meetings

The information transferred during formal and informal meetings provides a virtual reservoir of knowledge. It would be optimal if we could capture and retain this discourse for future analysis.

It is much easier to capture a formal meeting rather than informal. The formal meeting can be captured on video or audio. I recommend video because we are once again generating a library of face-to-face communications with all its subtleties. We could quickly generate vast libraries of knowledge and without the effective use of librarian functionality and technology this knowledge would quickly be relegated to the basement warehouse. Careful selection, categorization and storage of meeting materials are essential to its value. For now, recognize that the librarian functionality of attaching relevant Meta data to meeting contents is critical for its ability to be later retrieved.

Delivery systems can range from video libraries to web-enabled streaming media files. Either system needs to have a categorization methodology applied so the information can be searched and indexed and be returned as part of a knowledgebase search.

Knowledge time-off

3M realized early on that the bulk of its assets walked out the door at 5:00 every day. They decided to implement a knowledge time for employees that enabled their staff to take a one-hour break during every workday to work on any project they liked or thought up. Many ideas that had previously been shelved by managers took on a life of their own. Products such as yellow sticky notes and scotch tape are two of the "management scrapped" ideas that individual knowledge workers spearheaded themselves on the knowledge time-off.

Just as importantly, the knowledge management infrastructure 3M had built enabled one researcher to post information about a new type of adhesive he had invented and another to find the information and encapsulate that first idea into the yellow sticky note concept. One person was able to build on the ideas of another in a way that the original person never even thought about.

Another trait similar to the water cooler punishment is that of reading at ones desk. Managers in North America are often frustrated and contemptuous of anyone that reads at their desk. Many managers feel that any studying is secondary to "work" and should be performed on an employee's own time. I myself have been guilty of this in the past. Realize that if we cultivate the concept, that gaining knowledge is secondary to "real work", then we are undermining our overall intent of knowledge management.

Of course there must always be a balance. Some things will always take precedence over learning (such as when your wastepaper basket is on fire beside your desk).

HELP (Heuristic Enterprise Learning Program)

The concept behind HELP (Heuristic Enterprise Learning Program) is founded in the roots on knowledge brokering. We discussed in Chapter 1 the premise that people typically have an intrinsic desire to place a value on their Tacit knowledge and as such treat it as a commodity. We experience this in our everyday lives when we need to know something. We approach another individual (the seller) who we hope can provide us with some insight on a particular subject matter. The seller listens to the request, evaluates the individual requesting the knowledge (the buyer) and begins the process of mentally assessing the value of the knowledge in relation to the relationship with the buyer.

Trust is extremely important in the barter process because trust formulates the basis for an easy and immediate exchange. If the seller has experience with the buyer then the seller knows that if he/she sells the knowledge that there is a high likelihood that the buyer will reciprocate one day when the seller is in need of knowledge. This is the fastest form of negotiation.

If the buyer is not personally known but has a reputation that has preceded him for participating in knowledge exchange then the price is a little higher and introduces a little hesitation, but the transaction will likely go through. The buyer will be put in a sort of credit situation until the buyer has the chance to reciprocate and the seller can test the value of the credit. Often, key details may be withheld during the initial knowledge transaction and held in reserve until the credit can be put to the test. If the credit proves OK during the reciprocating transaction then further transactions should allow the free flow of knowledge without reservation.

If the buyer is unknown to the seller, and has no preceding reputation, or has a reputation for assuming credit for others knowledge, then the response to the request may be varied and unpredictable. Some sellers may outright refuse to transact, others may politely inform the buyer they don't have the knowledge or the time, others may demand public credit before proceeding, others (usually outside the organization) will place a monetary value on the knowledge. Typically, inside an organization, the monetary value of knowledge is negotiated during the hiring process and is renegotiated incrementally as a salary increase or performance bonus. There are many ways to respond to distrust and the higher the level of distrust the higher the price the seller sets on the commodity.

The reason a seller is willing to sell their product is also varied. Motivators are money, respect, notoriety, privilege, security, fear, etc... I don't feel we can isolate and develop systems for the myriad of reasons for sale. We can definitely build infrastructure to assist in the transactional process and help cultivate an environment where individuals can better assess and negotiate trust levels.

The final form of transaction is the knowledge broker that may not have the solution but may know of someone that does. This form of transaction is also dependent on trust level and the motivations for sale are also varied. This type of transaction is also an important part of a complete knowledge transfer system in organizations of any size.

HELP as a Knowledge Map and Accreditation System

Why do we what to build a HELP system? The answer is that the HELP system will build a dynamic enterprise knowledge map that identifies those individuals that are willing to participate in knowledge transfer as well as the areas in which they may offer Tacit knowledge on specific subjects.

So how can we develop a system using technology to facilitate knowledge transactions and trust negotiation?

The Heurist Enterprise Learning Program (HELP) is a methodology-based system. The 10-step method is as follows:

1. The system sends out an e-mail daily to all staff
2. Daily response is mandatory as part of staff's base job description
3. The e-mail asks 6 questions:
    - Did someone help you with a problem today?
    - If so, who?
    - Nature of the problem?
    - Nature of the solution?
    - Was the problem solved (completely, partially, not solved)?
    - If "Not Solved" was the seller able to refer someone else?
4. The response is parsed and results stored in a database
5. The buyer is awarded 3 credits for completing the form
6. The seller is awarded 20 credits for Solved, 10 for partial, 5 for referral
7. A search front-end is built to access the database
8. Buyers search the HELP knowledgebase to identify potential sellers

9. Seller information is available on-line so they can be located and engaged
10. The database is regularly analyzed to determine whom the buyers and sellers are, what areas of expertise they offer, the frequency of each participant and the level of skill of individual sellers to resolve problems and transfer their Tacit knowledge. Frequent use by individual buyers can also help point to areas where specific buyers may need additional training or support.

The results of analyzing the knowledge base can then be used to develop recognition programs based on earned credits. Rewards can range from public recognition to monetary bonuses or promotion.

Developing an enterprise scale knowledge map is a ferociously complex task given that Tacit knowledge continues to grow with experience and changes in environment and job functionality. Maintenance of a manual system is time consuming, expensive and prone to high levels of inaccuracy. By automating the process of knowledge map development and binding it back to one or more reward programs works well with the concept that individuals place value on their knowledge and expect to sell their knowledge.

The two most relevant questions in the e-mail are: Who provided help and the nature of the problem. The rest of the information is useful for analysis but the first two really build the foundation for the knowledge map. These two questions identify who the sellers are, how willing they are to participate, and the areas they are knowledgeable in.

Of course, the message delivery and retrieval system can really be anything that serves the same functionality. If you would prefer to have a message pop up on the screen of a mainframe terminal that collects the same information then the results will be the same. It is really the intent as opposed to the delivery mechanism.

The concept of HELP is not fool proof but is a lot more efficient and cost effective than the manual alternatives.

Gap Analysis

In the knowledge management undertaking we must always assess where we are and where we want to be. Knowing this, we can then perform a gap analysis to determine which pieces of the jigsaw puzzle we're missing.

When we know where we are and where we're going we can proceed to develop a road map that will guide us in required culture re-engineering, technology deployment, policies, processes and methodologies.

The gap analysis can then be bound to typical risk, issue, opportunity and change management controls and be encapsulated by the Trinity (scope, timeline and budget).

CHAPTER 7—
Project Management Framework

In Step 6 of my research map I suggest that you find out about the existence of a Project Management Framework in the enterprise.

When I fired off a draft of this book to my VP of sales for his comments, to my surprise, he responded with the question "What does this mean?" at the project management step. Now, I know he's familiar with projects but it was the framework part that I was failing to articulate.

Therefore, this chapter will explore the concept of a simple project framework, what is a framework, why we need one, and how it works. I had to make a decision that there was value in discussing this subject as there are ample books on project management on the market that describe simple to complex strategies for managing projects and this book is focused on knowledge management. But the bottom line is that a project management framework is really a formal methodology for collecting and disseminating both Explicit and Tacit knowledge.

The framework is relatively simple. It's broken into four concepts: The Trinity, Management Controls, Proxy Reporting and Post Implementation Review. I'll go over each one in turn. Before we begin, many of you reading this may have run projects in the past and may be wondering why I'm not talking about Waterfall Methodology, Iterative Processes or Rapid Development. These are methods of executing project staging over the life cycle of the project. Some methods are simply step-by-step, others require systematic feedback loops, and others leap ahead of the final deliverable by delivering pieces into production to test their viability throughout the development. These systems of project deployment are well documented and debated in project management journals everywhere and most importantly are all included in the Trinity. There's no need for me to decide which system is best as they all have a place in managing projects and any of them work within the scope of the Trinity.

The four framework components I'll speak of are used for measurement and communication.

The Trinity

The cornerstone of the four project management framework components is the Trinity.

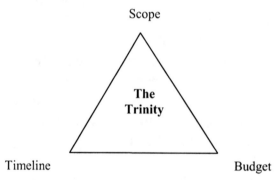

As the drawing indicates, the Trinity is concerned with putting a management wrapper around the three physical aspects of any project: the scope, timeline and budget.

Although the Trinity is extremely important for project managers it is far more important that everyone use this fundamental tool to manage their everyday projects of every size. It's simple and effective and makes people think before acting. Before anyone goes off and starts a project (small or large) it should be required that he or she file a Trinity plan with their manager. Even if it's on one piece of paper or a napkin, the real purpose is the process of actually writing down ones intentions and testing those intentions against a predetermined scope, budget and timeline. It makes people accountable for their actions.

Scope: Scope is the most important thing to focus on as a project manager. Scope "creep" is when your project starts as one thing and then blossoms into something else without anyone really paying attention to the ramifications. This is classic on large projects and in large organizations. Once someone gets some money approved for a project, others try to get other work done that really has little to do with the original project, and bleed funds from the project to pay for it. Others decide that certain features just "must" be added to take advantage of this or that opportunity and the feature list just grows and grows because the enhancements look so small and trivial that project members just agree to it. Eventually these minor enhancements aggregate into very significant time expenditures and the Trinity is blown.

So how do we manage scope?

1. Create an articulate vision statement
2. Define the business requirements
3. Create a detailed project plan with carefully defined deliverables
4. Carefully define Roles and Responsibilities
5. Bind the project under the watchful eye of the Management
6. Controls we will be talking about in this chapter.

Timeline: You track timelines for obvious reasons. For tracking a timeline you can use something like Microsoft Project. Scope creep most often generates Timeline deviations.

Budget: Another obvious thing you must track. This is where you define every single thing that is going to cost money during a project (I do mean everything). Once you've guessed at everything that could drain your coffers, you factor in a contingency amount to cover the costs you can't guess, as these will always appear. Budget deviations are most often generated by scope creep. Notice the similarity to time-line problems.

Management Controls

So why did I skip through the Timeline and Budget sections so quickly? Because you can learn that stuff anywhere. What's more important for knowledge management efforts are the Management Controls.

What are the management controls? Take a look at the following diagram and you'll see the flow of knowledge from one management control to the next:

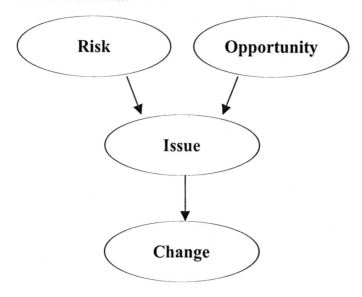

As you can see, Risks and Opportunities escalate to become Issues, and Issues escalate to Change management for resolution.

1. Risk Management

If you decide you don't want to use many different management controls and will only ever use one, than this is the one. This is where our Tacit knowledge comes shining through. Risk management is part of the formal project management framework and is designed to stimulate, escalate and capture risk-based tacit knowledge. At each stage of a risks life cycle we store its properties, state and assignments. These are retained in our knowledge management systems as a "lessons learned" library.

Risks are potentially harmful exposures that we forecast using our years of experience in determination of everything that can possibly go wrong, from the obvious to the subtle. Conditions in which the project exists, including political, demographic, and economic, etc. have an impact on your potential success or failure. Since change is constant, then our knowledge management concerns are to capture the risks and identify whoever has had experience with similar issues and may be able to offer input on how to resolve them.

Identifying our concerns well in advance gives us significant leverage to protect against them.

The process of Risk escalation is simple. Here's the rule of thumb:

1. If it's low risk then you just assign it and monitor it.
2. If it's medium risk then you assign it, monitor it and develop a contingency plan
3. If it's high risk, it escalates to a issue automatically and must be resolved right away

You can manage risks (and all the other controls as well) by using an automated program or you can use a simple logbook. It doesn't really matter so long as you manage it. Of course, from a knowledge management perspective it would be better to store this information digitally so it can participate in the knowledge base. Hard copy makes things very difficult to search and retrieve.

Microsoft Exchange is a particularly excellent product to build automated management controls upon because the asynchronous form-based workflow capabilities are exactly what management control escalation systems take full advantage of. You can also build a risk log MS Word or MS Excel spreadsheet document and store it on an Office 2000 server as a web page. You can also build a web-enabled application that uses a database back-end to store the information.

Whichever way you choose to develop and implement the management controls is much less important that enforcing their use through policy and training. It will obviously cost more initially to develop a database system as compared to a simple web document, but the long-term savings if you intend to use it for more than one project will be worth the time. Storing the data in Exchange public folders or in a database will allow you to write business rules into the logic that can perform the escalation automatically and forward the high-level issues to those that require the information. Your business rules become workflow rules that lend themselves very well to technologies such as web applications, Microsoft Exchange, Microsoft Office 2000 and directory services. We'll discuss these technologies in detail in Chapter 8.

Now that you have this information stored in a database it can participate in your knowledge map that I describe as the HELP system in Chapter 6.

Here is a sample risk log:

ITEM	The Item Number of the Risk being analyzed
RISK	The Risk being analyzed
S—Scope	What is the possibility of this Risk affecting the scope?
$—Budget	What is the possibility of this Risk affecting the budget?
T—Timeline	What is the possibility of this Risk affecting the timeline?
O—Opportunities	What is the possibility of this Risk affecting the opportunities?
R	The overall Rating of the Risk
L	**Low impact**—(Requires Monitoring—Project Proceeds)
M	**Medium Impact**—(Requires Contingency Plan—Project Proceeds)
H	**High Impact**—(Resolution Required Immediately)

Item	Risk	Date	S	$	T	O	R	Action Taken
1	Technology will change throughout the life of this project	7/15/99	M	M	M	M	M	Assigned to Bob. Develop contingency plan that will address the potential changes to technology and a strategy to minimize impact. Setup on-going monitoring.
2	Equipment may arrive late	7/15/99	L	M	H	L	H	Assigned to Mary. High risk because of weather conditions within the state. Late equipment delivery will defer deployment to branches.
3	Computer Room upgrades not completed on-time	7/19/99	L	M	H	L	M	Assigned to Jane. Contingency would be to build production machines in a different room and move in when completed. Power and cabling will be required in temporary room.
4	A Project team member may become absent or leave the project	7/30/99	L	L	L	L	L	Assigned to Jim. Identify additional resources to retrofit team when necessary.
5	Restricted IP address range not put in place by Dept. Y to allow mainframe traffic to access from Agency	9/2/99	H	H	H	L	H	Assigned to Frank. Dept. Y must be convinced to allow 10.X addresses to route across the state Intranet to access Dept. Y resources or else Agency will need to deploy firewalls to each branch at a cost of approximately $400,000.00
6	Dept. X not installing Exchange/GroupWise connector to facilitate system to system e-mail and calendar traffic	9/29/99	H	H	H	L	H	Assigned to Betty. Dept. X has stipulated that they would be ready in November to manage the connector portion of our connectivity. I haven't heard back from them since. I feel this will be a huge political roadblock.

2. Opportunity Management

Opportunity management is the inverse of Risk management. We can easily recognize that over the length of a large project things will change. This is especially true in the Information Technology field. As new products or revisions come available, as politics, economics and demographics change, we need to assess whether or not we should take advantage of the new change or will it set us back so much that it will significantly effect the Trinity.

The Opportunity log and/or program work exactly the same as the Risk log/program. The major difference is that Opportunities are not part of determination of a projects viability. In other words, we typically build a project on its own merits without assessing opportunities that don't exist. As opportunities come along we may or may not take advantage of them depending on how they effect the Trinity and their potential return. If we choose to ignore or never take advantage of an opportunity then the project is still viable. On the other hand if we choose to ignore a risk it could affect the viability of the entire project if it comes to fruition.

From a knowledge management perspective it is important to capture opportunities as they represent one of the most important aspects of knowledge management, the stimulation, identification and capturing of innovation in the enterprise.

Sometimes, throughout a project, we lose track of opportunities that present themselves without a systematic approach to opportunity management. Without a management system these opportunities will drift into nowhere and get forgotten. Building software to automate escalation of opportunities, to consolidate and report on opportunities, and to send reminders at specific times based on thresholds and events are ways we can capitalize on technology to participate in a knowledge management system. Capturing these thoughts into a formal database will preserve them for future reference. Capturing this type of innovative tacit knowledge also continues to build our knowledge map and identify the innovative thinkers in the enterprise.

3. Issue Management

Once a Risk or Opportunity gets a "High" rating it should automatically be escalated to become and Issue. Issues require resolution immediately.

The process of Issue Management is one of resolving potential or realized risks and opportunities. This is the stage where we apply all of our problem solving experience (our Tacit knowledge) to overcome obstacles and facilitate opportunities. From a knowledge management perspective, capturing the resolution thought process and capturing the nature of the proposed solution provide us with key enterprise indicators of who the experts in given areas are and the innovative thought processes used in problem resolution. This allows us to identify who can be used as a potential resource on future problems of a similar nature as well as providing us an archive of solutions.

How you resolve issues is the business of business. How we capture that process and knowledge is the business of knowledge managers.

4. Change Management

Change management is mission critical to maintaining the project Trinity. Once we've decided how to resolve an issue we need to formalize its impact to the Trinity and gain necessary approval to make the required changes in scope, timeline and budget. Who is responsible for approval and when it will take place is the responsibility of the change management process. This is less important for knowledge managers and more important to project integrity. We should capture this process and knowledge, as part of our project management frame-work program or log files.

The change management process itself is fairly simple. If an issue can't be resolved within a specific time frame it is escalated to the next respective change committee. Even if it is resolved it will still need to go to the respective change committee for proper approval and sign-off.

You typically have three change committees:

Tier 1—Change Committee

Who: Usually the project team members

Authority: Can authorize changes in scope that don't affect timeline or budget.

Tier 2—Change Committee

Who: Usually the project sponsor and project manager

Authority: Can authorize changes in scope and timeline that doesn't affect the budget.

Tier 3—Change Committee

Who: Usually the Board of Directors or Governance Board

Authority: Can authorize changes in scope, time-line or budget.

Each committee is assigned a specific response turn around time. If they fail to respond, then the issue is escalated. This also helps break political barriers that often develop during projects when two different departments or people have different objectives in mind.

Proxy Reporting

We've now covered the Trinity and Management controls which takes us to Proxy reporting as the third topic in project management.

Before I describe proxy reporting I'll describe the process of initializing a project.

Prior to commencement of any project there is always a proposal. The proposal usually states the vision of the project, its anticipated costs and the intended benefits. This is usually fairly conceptual and high-level, creating a broad-stroke perspective. Once we've drafted the proposal we need to find a sponsor. The sponsor is the person who will take the idea to the Board of directors and get approval and funding. The Board is not going to release all the funding required because this is just a concept at this stage and the total funding model hasn't been developed anyway. They are likely to approve only a limited amount of funds and time to complete the next stage of the project, the Feasibility Study.

It's at the feasibility study phase that we begin to engage the project framework. Usually we perform the feasibility in somewhat of an isolated mode that avoids disrupting the enterprise with communications about something that may not even happen. We take our most educated guesses about corporate impact and test them against what we know on a localized basis. There is usually a very limited time allocated to the feasibility and often this step may be outsourced to a third party to offer an objective perspective.

Regardless of who develops the feasibility, the result is delivered to the Project Sponsor who, in turn, delivers it to the Board. Should the Board agree with the feasibility they will then typically release funding for the next phase that we will call the Detailed Analysis Phase. At this stage the feasibility becomes a project. Now that we have a project we register it and assign it a project number. This is where the framework kicks in.

The Key to Successful Proxy Reporting:

*"In order for a project management framework to work, the fundamental components of the framework **MUST** become part of the base job descriptions of **everyone** in the enterprise."*

Most importantly, the management across the organization must have a simple process integrated into their daily job function that makes it **mandatory** they participate in the project communication system.

As part of the management job description they must be notified of, and review, any potential project that can affect their respective areas. Therefore, when the project is registered it is the responsibility of the Project Sponsor to formally advertise the existence of this new project and disseminate the required reading (the feasibility study at this point) to the rest of the management team within a specified time frame.

After they receive the feasibility study, it then becomes the mandated responsibility of the management team to review and respond to the Project Sponsor any risks, opportunities or issues they have or foresee with the project, within a specified time frame.

Here's where the proxy kicks in. ***"There must be an organizationally mandated rule that anyone not responding within the allotted time frames will be proxied."*** That's it! It's that simple. Too often politics are the reason so many projects fall prey to failure, over-runs or never get started. Proxy reporting circumvents the politics of delay and keeps the project timelines in sync.

As the project moves through its allotted phases, as each meeting takes place in the organization, as each decision is faced and multiple people need to be involved, Proxy reporting keeps the wheels of time commitment moving. You can use this for everything in your enterprise that needs to be agreed to in groups large or small when issues need to be resolved. Proxy reporting works! I use it in everything I do when managing projects. There is nothing like seeing the expression on someone's face when you tell him or her you made a decision on his or her behalf. You can bet they'll show up for the next meeting and the one after that.

Of course the one caveat is ***that the Board of Directors must mandate this as part of peoples base job descriptions***. There will likely be contracts in place between the organization and the management staff. If you try to invoke this without top-level commitment it will fail.

The following illustrations represent the order of communications.

Figure 1: The Board mandates the Project Management Framework to all staff

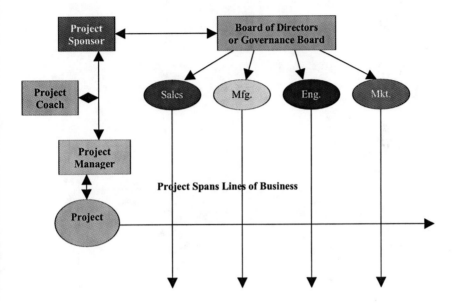

Figure 2: The project is registered and notification sent out

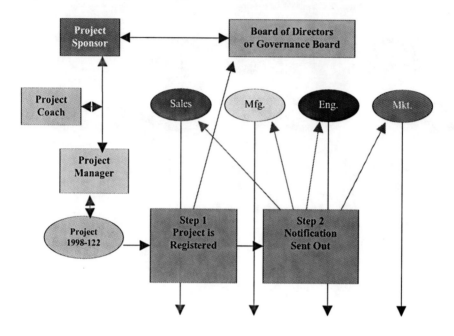

Figure 3: Feedback is required in specific time frame or participants are proxied.

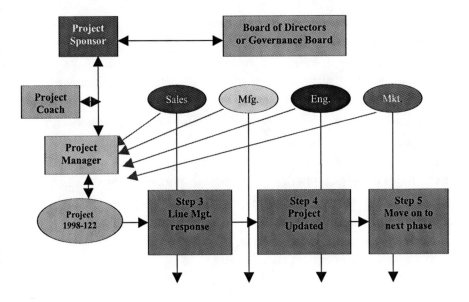

Post Implementation Review

The final component of the Project Management Framework is the Post Implementation Review or the "PIR" for short. The PIR is very important to the knowledge management effort because of its purpose within the project itself.

The purpose of the PIR is to get the project participants together at the end of the project to sit down and digest the project as a whole. It is during this stage that we analyze all the things that went wrong and all the things we did right. We document our problems in general and contemplate innovative ways to avoid these sorts of troubles in the future. We also document all the practices that proved most successful and contemplate ways to communicate these practices to other projects and people.

"The ability to capitalize on our successes, large and small, is the fundamental key to our survival."

The PIR takes place after the project is finished and therefore can't influence the project at all. What the PIR can do is capture the lessons learned into a formal knowledge management system so others can participate in the findings and experiences. This step is all too frequently avoided as it takes time, and most people have long since moved on to bigger and better things. It's important that project managers don't release project team members from this phase of the project responsibilities until the results are well documented and transferred into the knowledge base.

CHAPTER 8—
What are the Physical Infrastructure Components

We are faced with myriad technologies that can help us capture, analyze and transfer knowledge today, and the list just keeps on growing. In this section I intend to focus on Microsoft's solution offerings. I don't expect to hypothesize on every KM software solution under the sun, as the possible configurations and solutions are endless. Many may or may not have merit. I will only speak of what I have done and what I know works.

I work mostly with Microsoft products for the simple reason that they provide me almost anything I need or can think of: from operating systems to communications, from server and desktop applications to the development languages themselves. I tend to favor any infrastructure that supports COM (Component Object Model) based applications because COM standards are designed with code reusability in mind. Microsoft is a large advocate of COM and their products afford me many opportunities to exploit code written by developers a lot better than myself. I don't want to reinvent the wheel if one already exists; I just want to get at the data, information and knowledge in the easiest and least costly fashion. I also believe strongly in buying into a philosophy as opposed to a specific product. There is a greater chance the philosophy will be around longer than any product.

Knowledge Management Tools

Microsoft Site Server

Microsoft's Site Server product is really a suite of products as opposed to a singular product. For this book we are mostly interested in its Knowledge Manager and directory services components.

The Knowledge Manager that comes with Site Server really offers three levels of functionality:

1. It allows users to publish information;

   a. Content Management—means that multiple content authors can submit, tag, and edit content with a drag-and-drop Web interface. Site editors can then approve, edit, and enforce uniform guidelines for content.

   b. Content Deployment—means that knowledge managers can collect content for review on a staging server, and then deploy it to destination Web servers securely, reliably, and quickly. Deploy content across a single server or to multiple servers, as well as to UNIX-based servers.

2. Allows users to search for information across your organization

   a. Searching—means users can use the robust and powerful enterprise search server to find information in a range of sources—intranet and Internet Web sites, files, ODBC databases, and Exchange Server folders.

3. Deliver filtered, focused information and provide statistics

    a. Knowledge Manager—Users can easily browse, search, share, and subscribe to relevant information with a centralized Web-based application that integrates the Site Server knowledge management features.

    b. Personalization—Delivers personalized content on Web sites. Administrators can author personalized pages with the new Rule Builder tools. Use the Direct Mailer tool to build targeted mailings.

    c. Push—Microsoft Active Channel Server builds, manages, and schedules the delivery of organized and timely information. Active Channel Multicaster saves valuable network bandwidth by using multicast technology to deliver channels.

    d. Analysis—Generate reports that accurately reflect site usage. Classify Web site usage data and integrate other information to develop a more complete and meaningful profile of site visitors and their behavior. Enterprise management capabilities provide the ability to centrally administer complex, multihomed, or distributed server environments.

The ability for Site Server to categorize both structured and unstructured information gives us a powerful knowledge management tool that fits into a multi-tiered publishing approach that many organizations require. Often people wish to publish information to a knowledge base but haven't taken the steps to categorize or pre-qualify the information. Using Site Server we can have users publish information to preliminary test (staging) servers. From there, the postings can be moderated by knowledge managers to make sure that the content and the presentation both adhere to corporate standards and requirements.

The powerful search engine can parse through almost any type of data to retrieve, categorize and present relevant information in a timely fashion. The search engine can span across the corporate Intranet or reach across the Internet and index other web servers where pockets of valuable information can reside. Site server is the tool to use for indexing if you use more than one Microsoft Office 2000 server. Office 2000 uses its internal index server and can't span more than a single server. Site Server can index them all, allowing selective global indexing while Office 2000 provides local indexing.

The knowledge manager also participates in the construction, maintenance and deployment of a site wide vocabulary as we spoke of in Chapter 5.

Internet Locator Service (ILS) is an optional component of Microsoft Site Server that creates a dynamic directory of Microsoft NetMeeting users. From this directory, participants can locate each other on the Internet or corporate intranets for real-time conferencing and collaboration.

ILS offers a standards-based, dynamic directory solution for finding users on the Internet. It provides organizations with a directory server for NetMeeting users and provides a memory-resident database for storing dynamic directory information. For example, users can find dynamic information, such as an Internet Protocol (IP) address, for people currently logged on to an Internet service or site. The ILS database maintains the entries, which clients refresh periodically. This process ensures that clients can always access the most current information about each user's Internet location.

Traditional static directories contain information that is presumed to have value until it is removed. In contrast, the NetMeeting directory information quickly degrades over time because NetMeeting is an IP-based conferencing program. With the widespread use of Dynamic Host Configuration Protocol (DHCP), each time a user logs on to a local area network (LAN) or Internet service provider (ISP), the user's computer is assigned a different IP address, which means that the directory information needs to be frequently updated. Therefore, a traditional static directory approach cannot be used.

NetMeeting directory requirements resulted in ILS, the LDAP-based dynamic directory service. ILS information can be updated as frequently as needed because storage is not based on SQL or file-based databases. Instead, ILS stores directory data in memory. Even though the directory stores information differently, access to the information is still the same as traditional static directories. Therefore, NetMeeting uses LDAP to access the ILS server.

Microsoft NetMeeting

Microsoft Windows NetMeeting is changing the way people communicate and work together on the Internet and on corporate intranets. With its rich set of audio, video, and data conferencing features, NetMeeting has proven its effectiveness for management groups, developers, and user communities worldwide. NetMeeting is an extremely viable face-to-face facilitation tool.

NetMeeting is a powerful tool that allows real-time communication and collaboration over the Internet or corporate intranet. From a computer running Windows 95, Windows 98, or Windows NT 4.0, users can communicate over a network with real-time voice and video technology. Users can work together on virtually any Windows-based program, exchange or mark up graphics on an electronic whiteboard, transfer files, or use the text-based Chat program.

NetMeeting helps small and large organizations take full advantage of their corporate intranet for real-time communications and collaboration. On the Internet, connecting to other NetMeeting users is made easy with the Microsoft Internet Locator Service (ILS), which is an optional component of Site Server, allowing participants to call each other from a dynamic directory within NetMeeting or from a Web page. New features include Remote Desktop Sharing, virtual conferencing using Microsoft Outlook, new security features, and the ability to embed the NetMeeting user interface in corporate intranet Web pages.

Designed for corporate communication, NetMeeting supports international communication standards for audio, video, and data conferencing. With NetMeeting, people can communicate and collaborate with users of NetMeeting and other standards-based, compatible products. Users can connect by modem, Integrated Services Digital Network (ISDN), or local area network (LAN) using Transmission Control Protocol/Internet Protocol (TCP/IP). In addition, support for system policies in NetMeeting makes it easy for administrators to centrally control and manage the NetMeeting work environment.

Microsoft Office 2000

Document management is a large part of knowledge management. Much of what we interact with on a daily basis is unstructured knowledge in the form of documents. These documents include word processing documents, spreadsheet documents and presentation documents such as Microsoft PowerPoint.

These documents are generated on stand alone workstations for the most part and are stored in a variety of locations that include local workstation hard drives, file servers, CDRom drives, tape back-up devices and web servers. There are other locations such as floppy disks, microfiche and hard copy paper archives but floppies are rapidly becoming a thing of the past and paper based archives are too slow, so many organizations are choosing to digitally scan archived papers and microfiche to provide on-line search and retrieve capabilities.

For documents that are generated using typical office productivity applications such as those in the Microsoft Office suite, Microsoft has created the newest flavor of its Office suite called Office 2000. The biggest difference between older versions of Microsoft Office and Office 2000 are the server-side components. Microsoft developed a web enabled back-end storage facility for its Office suite that sits on top of Microsoft's Internet Information Server (Microsoft web server software). The Office 2000 server-side components enable documents from any of the Office 2000 suite of applications to publish, search, retrieve and collaborate across an enterprise Intranet or across the global Internet. Office 2000 server components also install a smaller version of Microsoft's SQL 7.0 database in order to hold on-line discussions on top of or imbedded within the documents themselves. Organizations can chose to install the full version of SQL 7.0 if they intend to have more than ten concurrent discussions going on at one time.

The discussion component is extremely valuable as you can hold discussions on documents anywhere that can be reached by your web browser. This way individuals within your enterprise, that belong to your discussion server, can hit any web site they have access too around the world and start a threaded conversation on top of or within the document or web page. Other individuals that belong to the same discussion server will see and can participate in the discussions on the local or remote web sites just by hitting the same page and turning on discussions in their browser.

Because the Office 2000 back-end components sit on top of Microsoft's web server, it is therefore a web server just like any other and can be viewed, browsed, searched and presented like any other web site. This makes users interface into the system a familiar web browser, significantly decreasing training costs and issues.

Microsoft has developed a philosophy that I agree with whole-heartedly. They commit to the concept of providing a universal front-end into everything. Using the Office 2000 suite of applications that include MS Word (Word Processor), MS Excel (Spreadsheet), MS PowerPoint (Presentation), MS Access (Database), MS Outlook (E-mail Client) and MS Internet Explorer (Web Browser) means that we only have to deploy and support one suite of applications. More importantly, we can utilize the same suite of tools to access any digital resource in the enterprise.

It no longer matters that you may run an SAP, Oracle or SQL 7.0 back-end. We use the Office 2000 suite of applications to interface to middleware COM engines that provide all the necessary work to input and extract the right information. Office 2000 applications provide the presentation. This functionality also simplifies deployment issues significantly. We typically desire to avoid visits to the end user workstations as much as possible because of the huge costs associated with personal technician visits and the disruptions and training requirements for the end users.

Office 2000 server components also introduce us to Web Folders for the first time. Up to now we typically create a "drive map" to a conventional file server. This is a virtual connection to a server using protocols that are only desirable on Local Area Networks. These same drive maps present significant technological, performance and security hurtles when you need to connect over the Internet (which is quickly becoming the preferred method). Microsoft has introduced its Web Folders as a method of establishing virtual connections to folders on an Office 2000 file server using web-based protocols. This is very important because these protocols are both designed to operate on the web very efficiently as well as providing the necessary security inter-actions that are typically required to participate with firewalls and other security devices. To the users this means that they can log onto the Internet anywhere and open Web Folders on their desktop and transparently interact with documents or anything else they've stored in the folders.

Now that we have all the functionality and convenience we could ask for to get access to and publish our documents to a web-based server, the functionality of the server's Indexing service continually searches through the server's folder structures and indexes all the information within the documents as well as the Meta Data that was stored when someone enters information in the properties section of the document. Office 2000 server software then presents a web page for users to access, search and retrieve the information they desire.

The Office 2000 server setup can be performed in one day. This is an excellent example how some knowledge management components can be put into action with little effort. The larger effort is deploying Office 2000 to the desktops you expect to participate. The major dif-ference between the deployment of older versions of Office and Office 2000 is that the Office 2000 product provides an extremely powerful deployment resource kit to allow the deployment team to custom con-figure virtually every aspect of Office and push the installation out from the server. The installed client then references back to the server whenever it needs something or someone runs the auto-repair features. This saves organizations tremendous on-site diagnostic costs as users that experience technical difficulties can tell the system to repair itself, and for the most part it does. Of course it won't recover deleted or lost end-user data but then again if the software did everything Microsoft would never sell another upgrade.

This technology doesn't consume any additional bandwidth from your network than you are consuming at the moment (in fact it will probably decrease as a result of the efficient web-based protocols) but you will find added latency in storing and retrieving your files from Web Folders when you are connected to a high speed Local Area Network (LAN) connection. The reason for the added delay is that traditional drive mappings use a protocol call RPC that is designed specifically for computer-to-computer communications on fast networks. The use of HTTP or HTTP/S in Office 2000 Web Folders introduces more overhead to the systems that are communicating. The delay is noticeable, so this part of the technology should be included in your "user expectation setting" efforts.

One big benefit of using web-based protocols is that you can choose to deploy a Digital Certificate on the Office 2000 web server and activate digital encryption. This will encrypt any of the information going to or from the server. Encryption does degrade performance of servers because of the additional number crunching required but a decent server will barely even notice it.

In Chapter 8 "Developing a Pilot Program" I use the deployment of Office 2000 as a simple case example. If your interest is document knowledge collaboration you will wish to review that chapter as well.

Microsoft Exchange

E-mail plays a vital role in today's efforts to disseminate information. "Exchange Server" is Microsoft's e-mail messaging platform. The reason e-mail is so effective in communications is because it is so prevalent in today's digital world and offers users a chance to communicate asynchronously. The problem with e-mail is that it doesn't lend itself well to management. Most e-mail information is deemed ephemeral and is purged after reading. We typically don't archive or chronicle this information. Therefore, knowledge management efforts need to be directed to developing e-mail systems that capture, categorize and archive the flow of thought that transpires throughout the life of a particular e-mail thread (conversation).

Exchange provides tools embodied within its system that allow knowledge managers to store discussion-based information in Public Folders. These public folders are server-side repositories that can have rules and actions applied to them that allow these asynchronous discussions to be captured and preserved for future analysis. The public folders can also be bound to enterprise forms (expense reports, timesheets, etc.) that are developed within the Exchange and associated client (Outlook 2000) environment. These forms capture information that is entered into them and transports the information in the form of a MAPI message (e-mail). Developers can then write extremely sophisticated programs that can parse through e-mails, extract the required information and perform virtually any task you desire on the data. This information can be stored off to a database or used to respond in predetermined formats.

The ability to automate and manipulate the e-mail data enables knowledge managers to develop complex workflow systems that build form and structure around the way we work and interact on a daily basis. An example would be the use of an expense report form. Users would open a new expense report form in their e-mail client (Outlook) and fill in the required information. This form would then be submitted to a public folder. A server-side program would fire off when the new message arrives in the Public Folder and would read the contents into a database. Depending on who sent in the form, the server-side program could lookup who the initiators manager is from the global address list that is part of Exchange. Another form could then be sent to the manager requesting approval of the first persons expense report. If the manager is away that week the program could time-out if the message isn't opened within a specific time and look up the managers boss from the same global address list and forward it on to that person. You get the idea.

Exchange participates in COM-based application development and can therefore integrate in extremely complex parallel and serial work-flow systems. There is virtually no limit to what knowledge managers can accomplish when Exchange is integrated into other components of the Microsoft BackOffice suite (which includes most of the technologies we are discussing in this chapter). The benefit is also aligned with Microsoft's and my philosophy we discussed earlier of using a single user interface (Office 2000) as the portal into much more complex back-end systems.

Exchange can also set up Public Folders to simply capture threaded discussions and provides users the ability to search and sort through historical e-mail conversations to find jewels of conversational wisdom from the past.

Microsoft Exchange also makes it possible to host on-line meetings, conduct real-time discussions with co-workers, business partners and customers, and collaborate on documents and projects on-line in real time. To facilitate these activities Microsoft Exchange includes the **Microsoft Exchange Chat Service**, and the **Internet Locator Server (ILS)**. The Chat Service is an IRC server capable of hosting 10,000 simultaneous users for real-time chats. Users can participate in chats using any IRC or IRCX client. In addition, the Chat Service can be added to an Active Server page, making it part of a more comprehensive Web-based application.

The Internet Locator Server (ILS) tracks who is on-line and ready to participate in collaborative activities such as collaborating on documents, participating in whiteboard discussions, or video conferencing via Microsoft NetMeeting. Because ILS is included with Microsoft Exchange a user can go to the Microsoft Exchange directory, select a name, and initiate a NetMeeting, eliminating the need to maintain separate address books. Similarly an administrator is not forced to maintain a separate directory for messaging and collaboration.

The ability to use Exchange as a participant in a knowledge management effort makes it a key component in your overall knowledge management campaign.

Microsoft SQL Server

It's almost impossible to use computers and not have some sort of interaction with a database now and then. Databases are warehouses for structured information. When we clearly understand the nature of the information we need to capture, in respect to the type, size and quantity we can develop cellular repositories that can hold similar pieces of data. These pieces can then be related to others if the requirement exists by developing relationships between the different data types. Collectively these become databases. Even a spreadsheet is a type of database although it presents a more free form approach to structure.

Microsoft's SQL Server product is the enterprise scale database system that can hold as little or as much data as required depending on hardware and performance constraints. SQL (System Query Language) is the language we use to access the database.

SQL 7.0 comes with the knowledge management tools we need to provide serious analysis on the structured data held in the database repository. The knowledge management tools available to us allow us to store structured information extracted from most types of data stores and model the data as we see fit for our purposes. This modeling functionality is called Data Warehousing and allows us to build matrixes of data, index the data, perform calculations on the data, and present views to our users so they can see they data they wish to view from many different perspectives.

An analogy would be to extrapolate accounting history information on sales and blend the data with pipeline information on sales projections from the sales department to analyze and build a view of sales forecast information based on historical trending for the sales department. The accounting department can also see the data but they may want a different view based on the actual vs. projected numbers for budgeting purposes.

Databases provide the structured back-end for enterprise management systems, executive reporting systems, personal information managers, accounting systems and a host of other applications. The data we can pull, analyze and present can be accessed through a web browser running on a the corporate intranet or global Internet as well as be integrated into virtually any other application we decide to build. The information can also be presented back through standard office applications like Office 2000 to maintain that single user interface we spoke of earlier.

Because of the complexity of building both a database and a data warehouse, you will need a high level of skill-set in your staff to both design and implement such knowledge management solutions. The

costs for development vary based on the complexity of the requirements. The typical costs for a data warehouse run quite high because
of the skill-set requirement and the system requirements. System
requirements usually demand robust, powerful hardware, as the indexing and reporting functions are extremely hardware intensive.

Often at times we desire to extract information from outside sources
or sources of data that we cannot rely on the quality of the data.
Therefore additional efforts in time and resources may be required to
"scrub" the inbound data to ensure a certain level of data integrity. The
type and structure of data from some systems will also typically not
match the type and structure of our desired system. Therefore, data
translation mechanisms must be purchased as packaged software
requiring configuration or be custom developed. These steps also add
significant cost and time to the knowledge management project.
Microsoft's SQL 7.0 fortunately comes with a powerful data translation component that greatly reduces development efforts in this area.

Microsoft Systems Management Server

If your knowledge management efforts also require internal knowledge on performance, inventory or technology forecasting for budgets
then Microsoft's System Management Server (SMS) provides the
tools necessary to analyze the existing systems in your enterprise.

Knowledge management often extends into the help desk, as help desk
analysts require repeated access to the knowledgebase in efforts to
support their clients. SMS provides them the ability to query physical
configurations and components throughout an enterprise to assist them
in problem determination and solution building.

Accounting departments can query the hardware and software inventory reports from SMS to analyze the current quantities, types, configurations and usage of technological resources.

The IT section can monitor software usage using SMS's license metering services. This tells them activity levels on software and allows them to purchase software license based on usage as opposed to buying individual copies for everyone's machine offer the opportunity for significant cost savings.

SMS offers many other tools and additional functionality but these are the components significant to knowledge management.

Microsoft Proxy Server

Many of the tools we use today take advantage of the Internet as the communication medium to collect and disseminate knowledge. Being connected to the Internet means that anyone around the globe can gain access to our most valuable resource, our knowledge. Therefore we need to address the idea of security in every aspect of what we do in knowledge management.

Microsoft's Proxy Server product provides a firewall between the internal users and external Internet users. This security wall also comes with knowledge tools that allow us to collect statistics on usage. The statistics are weak and other products like Microsoft Site Server provide much more robust reporting mechanisms that can be used in conjunction with Proxy Server to tract an individual users access throughout a system. Tracking user activity allows you to analyze the strengths and weaknesses of how we are presenting our web-enabled knowledge.

This section is included to show you one of many different types of security systems that can and should be employed in the knowledge management infrastructure to protect your knowledge assets. It also demonstrates that even security products can be used to extract pieces of knowledge that can be used by many people in their knowledge efforts.

ListServ—from L-Soft International Inc.

Here one place I'll deviate from the Microsoft platform. We've talked briefly in the section on Microsoft Exchange about discussions. Here we'll drill down on this some more because this is one of those gray area tools that somewhat broaches Explicit and tacit knowledge management.

Yes, I know you've heard me time and time again talking about tacit knowledge as requiring face-to-face communications. Why? Because I say that face-to-face communications is the best vehicle to establish the required level of trust to enable the brokering of Tacit knowledge. Why then do I feel that the ListServ product can participate in Tacit knowledge management?

One reason I choose ListServ, or any product that offers the same functionality, is that I can firstly categorize my discussion by topic prior to the conversation taking place. What I mean by this is that users choose a topic they wish to collaborate on, start a threaded e-mail conversation and send their replies into that specific topic repository. Knowledge managers can establish the discussion headings in advance, such as using the vocabulary we designed in Chapter 5. They can also start discussion groups on projects or areas of specialization. The key is, you're not restricted at the outset as to how you want to configure the top-level discussion topics, this is fully configurable.

Another important reason I feel that ListServ functions on the Tacit side of knowledge management is that you can define security around each discussion independently as well as being able to moderate the content posted into the ListServ to provide filtering if required. This is very important if project or team members have already established their trust level and are fully willing to disseminate their thought process into a threaded e-mail repository. This gives participants a sense of security that their knowledge will not be broadcast to the ends of the earth. What's important to knowledge managers is that the discourse that takes place is text based, easily archived and can be accessed at a later date.

Now that the discussions are archived ListServ provides a web-based search engine that allows security privileged users to search the knowledgebase with ease. The interface allows discussions to be fully indexed in a variety of ways and delivered in a format that allows participants to be able to "walk" up and down an entire conversation thread so they can read the evolution of the problem all the way to the nature of the solution. This gives the reader a good impression of the thoughts that substantiate the discussion.

As I said, Listserv, or any similar product, only participates partially. The reason I say this is that e-mail is far too impersonal and has a tendency to allow its users to shortcut a lot of the nuances that relay volumes of information gained during face-to-face conversations. You're also never really sure if someone knows something or they are "hitting the marketing literature" in-between replies.

The bottom line is that ListServ serves a valuable purpose and is an excellent, inexpensive tool to work with. It can be installed and be up and running in a day and training is simple e-mail and/or a web browser. User participation is also easily measured by volume of input. It takes time for people to get used to the system but once they catch on it can really heat up the exchange of knowledge in your enterprise.

The data can be stored in ListServ's proprietary compressed flat file system or stored in a database of your choosing so the data is available for integration into other systems. The choice is yours and I highly recommend this as an enterprise tool.

XML (Extensible Markup Language)

I need to discuss XML in this section as it is destined to play an important role in the infrastructure for knowledge management.

XML is a markup language for documents containing structured information. Structured information contains both content (words, pictures, etc.) and some indication of what role that content plays (for example, content in a section heading has a different meaning from content in a footnote, which means something different than content in a figure caption or content in a database table, etc.). Almost all documents have some structure.

A markup language is a mechanism to identify structures in a document. The XML specification defines a standard way to add markup to documents.

So what would we use XML for?

If we look at the way we traditionally priced products and services in the past we would see that we would typically determine our costs, figure out the profit margin we wanted and those variables determine what we would sell our products or services for. Nowadays though, we are leaning more towards determining what the consumer will pay and use that as our common starting point to determine what our acceptable costs can be.

Now we know how much money can be allocated to costs, we need to start accounting for every single cost that is involved in delivery. This doesn't mean just inside our own company but the costs presented to us by suppliers and distributors as well. Therefore we need to get the costing information from our downstream and upstream partners to develop our over-all costing model.

Now we are faced with a problem. There is a very high likelihood that our upstream and downstream partners use completely different accounting systems and will be religious in their commitment to their accounting solutions. So how do we consolidate our information from tens or hundreds of partners?

In the past twenty to thirty years' major corporations have used EDI (Electronic Data Interchange) as the translation system between disparate accounting systems. EDI presents each partner with a set of standard electronic documents (forms) that each accounting system has to "port" its data to. In other words, the standard EDI document will need a map to be developed that connects one particular field in the accounting system (such as "purchase order number") to the standard purchase order number field in the EDI document. The same has to be done again at the other end so the data can be taken out of the EDI document and inserted into the other partners accounting system.

The need for an extremely high degree of accuracy in delivery and data integrity has led to the creation of VAN's (Value Added Networks) that can guarantee this level of delivery services. This has been technologically effective but traditionally only the largest of companies can actually afford these services as the costs of development of maps, costs of the VAN's and cost of maintenance is extremely high. The structure of the EDI documents is also totally inflexible or it wouldn't be a standard. But even the large corporations are now being faced with these significant costs as they now begin moving their costing strategy to the system based on what consumers are willing to pay first. Additionally, because of these high EDI costs, even the large companies lose out on tracking "every" cost, as smaller companies that may participate in the over-all costing model can't afford to participate electronically. Therefore, the total costing model is never complete and therefore unmanageable.

So how do we resolve this issue? The answer at this point in time and for the next few years at least is XML. Because of the flexible and easily understood nature of the XML language it allows developers to build translation systems between systems that can be very customized, take full advantage of low cost communication networks (such as the Internet) and completely cut out the VAN's used in EDI. Using XML we can reach into one system and take a "snapshot" of the data we want to share and pass the entire recordset to the partner who imports the data using XML as well. Very efficient, very clean and very low cost in comparison to EDI.

XML finally gives even the smallest of companies the chance to participate in the downstream and upstream costing process. The low cost of development, deployment and maintenance significantly lowers the overall costing model of all products and services that participate.

Communications

We've spoken of software tools to facilitate knowledge management, so now lets direct our attention to the communication highway that binds the enterprise. I won't dwell on the merits of one technology or another (such as Ethernet or Token-Ring) as it really doesn't matter to knowledge management how we get the information, only that it is accessible and delivered in a timely fashion.

Directory Services

Every organization has at least one directory. Every time you log onto your computer it checks a directory to see who you are and what you have rights to access. This is one type of directory. The type of directory I want to discuss from the knowledge management perspective is a distributed directory that can hold variable data as well as be accessed by multiple systems. The network logon directory I just spoke of is usually proprietary to the network operating system manufacturer. The type of directory I want to talk about is an open standard and can be accessed by anyone or any software that has the right privileges and uses the right protocol.

The directory is called X.500. The organization that developed this standard is the International Standards Organization (ISO). X.500 has been around for many years now but is typically used only in large organizations because it is a very large and complex standard that embodies a total directory solution. The problem up to now has not only been its level of complexity but the software required on the client is also big and machine-intensive.

Recently the IT community, and especially the Internet Engineering Task Force (IETF) have developed a quicker, lighter version of one part of the standard called LDAP (Lightweight Directory Access

Protocol. There is little directory structure defined in the specification so users have the ability to craft their own directory structure. This is both good and bad. The good part is that nobody is telling you how the directory should look so you can be as inventive as the protocol allows. The bad part is that you can build a proprietary schema (directory structure) and it will have difficulties blending to other LDAP directories if the need arises (merger, acquisition, sale, etc.). X.500 on the other hand provides for a global definition of the directory and forces you to adhere to the global naming conventions. This is great if you buy another X.500 based company but usually doesn't happen on smaller scales. For the most part an LDAP directory is good enough for the average company.

Lightweight Directory Access Protocol (LDAP) is a standard method for program clients to query and access information stored on directory servers over Transmission Control Protocol/Internet Protocol (TCP/IP) connections. Typically, a published directory contains static data about people or other entities that users can access, for example, a telephone directory or e-mail address book.

LDAP is derived from the X.500 global directory and the Directory Access Protocol (DAP), a complex access protocol for performing a wide variety of directory functions. LDAP, a streamlined adaptation of DAP, does not need to support the unnecessary features of client-server access scenarios. The result is simplified implementation, reduced software complexity, improved performance, and wider adoption.

From the knowledge managers perspective this enterprise ubiquitous directory allows knowledge managers to store and replicate common knowledge throughout an enterprise. This means that information such as customer profiles, names, addresses, and telephone numbers etc. can be stored once and shared automatically via the LDAP protocol.

The information can be categorized and broken into logical units for replication to relevant points in an organization. This not only provides a consistent source of common data but provides any application development efforts the ability to tap into the central repository of common data (typically referred to as Common Intake).

The client side component is lightweight and pervasive in the industry. It is embedded in Web Browsers and can be embedded into new client software after first learning the LDAP protocol language.

Directories are both an excellent utility for storing, retrieving and replicating common data as well as being a universal storage mechanism for programmers.

On the down side, directories also require significant planning efforts and require programmers to learn the LDAP protocol. Breaking data into pieces that are distributed between a typical database and a directory also complicates data relationship building and requires significant monitoring of data integrity. These are both hurdles that can be overcome programmatically but they are still hurtles that must be accounted for in the desire to move knowledge into a directory.

Bandwidth Requirements

When we talk about communications with knowledge management in mind we first want to ascertain our lowest common denominator.

If we are focused on the face-to-face communications of Tacit knowledge than we need to review the types of technologies we expect to deploy to facilitate this type of communication. As we spoke of in Chapter 6—Virtual Teams, we could utilize a desktop video conferencing unit like Microsoft's NetMeeting. This product has the ability to operate over low speed modems, and if our lowest common denominator is analog technology (modems) or ISDN than we are pretty much restricted to this type of interface. If we could provide better bandwidth for the client-to-client conversations than we could still use the same product and achieve better clarity in the transmitted video signal.

On the other hand, if we intend to utilize some other video based technology we will need to ensure we have better bandwidth availability (such as fractional T1, T1, T3 or ATM line speeds or broadband communication links. These will typically start at 384 kb/sec and grow to extremely high speeds (1.5—100's of Mega bits per second). The broadband analog systems used by the cable television industry provide channels in 10 MHz increments such as watching a specific channel on television. You can transmit many channels on the same cable because they are all separated by a buffer frequency to avoid signal overlap.

The rule of thumb is *"never scrimp on bandwidth"*. The cost of bandwidth is coming down everyday with no end in site. The demands for bandwidth are constantly growing. This means you should build the biggest communication highway (pipe) you can (within technological and budget constraints) between any two given locations in your organization.

The Internet is rapidly growing as the cheap bandwidth carrier for all types of information. If your goal is quality though, you may desire to build a private network where you can guarantee quality of service. The Internet is a shared system and you can't guarantee that your packets won't get "bumped" (rejected) if the Internet routers get to busy with traffic overload. If some of your video or audio packets are bumped you may lose your synchronization signal that keeps your picture steady or keeps your voice from "popping". If you have to build your own network than ATM will provide the optimum level of quality of service. Other technologies such as Ethernet and Token-ring just don't have the ability built into the protocol to prioritize one type of service over another. That is exactly what ATM was designed from the ground up to provide.

Gap Analysis

The final step in assessing your physical infrastructure components is to determine the type of technologies you want to utilize, determine the potential effects of the technologies on your existing hardware, determine the lowest common denominator in network bandwidth and determine what levels of each you require to support your knowledge management requirements. Once you've determine the above then you can cost analyze the required upgrades and develop a project plan to implement them.

CHAPTER 9—
Developing a Pilot Program

As in most projects we always want to test and prove our concepts on a group of guinea pig users. In my project management framework I call these users "Early Adopters". You can call them anything you want but they are typically volunteers who are patient enough and willing to provide the necessary objective feedback to offer value to the project.

For knowledge management efforts I would usually begin with the IT staff as early adopters because they are usually well conditioned to changes in their environment and recognize the value of detailed feedback. IT people are also typically used to high levels of interaction (great for testing Tacit systems) and have very rigid processes (excellent source of Explicit knowledge) that lend themselves well to being captured in a KMS. The other value of using IT personnel is that they are much more intimate with computers and communications and can often support themselves, providing and documenting diagnostic and support steps along the way.

Your early adopter group should be limited to six people because of the rationale provided by the AT&T example we spoke of in chapter 6—Team Size.

Once you've chosen your team then we need to pick the system that focuses on the vision statement objectives (either building for Explicit, Tacit or both).

Let's assume the vision statement states that we want to capture unstructured document information and capture threaded conversations to collaborate on top of each document. Your steps would be:

1. Develop a project plan
2. Get a commitment on budgetary requirements
3. Assign the required human resources
4. Review the plan with project participants
5. Build a server-sizing document that analyses the storage, CPU, power, backup and disaster recovery, etc. requirements for Office 2000 server components and user data.
6. Design a security model for the server
7. Design a folder structure that synchronizes with the site vocabulary
8. Design a template document for consistency and publish its location
9. Build the server
10. Assign permissions
11. Deploy Office 2000 to the pilot desktops
12. Setup the browser discussions to point to the server
13. Setup web folders to the folder structure
14. Develop and implement a user training program
15. Implement test and feedback processes

Not as complex as you may have thought? You're right; the technological aspect is relatively simple for specific implementations of knowledge management. They can also get much more complex. I highly recommend you start small to get a flavor of the technologies, the processes and the cultural modification requirements and achieve small successes as you continue to implement additional systems. If you start too big, the project gets very complex quickly, produces very little in visible deliverables for money being spent and stands a much greater chance of failure.

Remember that the concept of capturing this knowledge may be desired but hasn't yet been proven as viable in your organization. Success must be measured in usage as opposed to effectiveness in deployment. Now that it is up and running you need to develop a program that encourages people to use it over extended periods of time, even after the novelty has worn off.

Commitment to the system is everything. Many KM projects begin with the best of intentions but suffer the fate of offering sizzle but no steak. It's the content that counts, not the cool technology. If you can't convince people to participate and create a fundamental desire for them use the system then you fail. I would then recommend going back to interoffice memos and using the telephone.

Your team feedback is essential. Is the interface too complex? Is the data stored where they would expect to find it or do they need to hunt and peck? Is it too slow? How can we make it easier, better or faster? There are many questions to ask and the replies should be used to tune the system to provide the portal the users really want to collaborate through. You also need to be constantly asking the questions: "Do our clients value this service?" and "How much are they willing to pay for this value (even if it is only time)?"

After it is tuned as well as it can be, what type of reward programs and refresher training do you need to continually reinforce participation? Will you measure your staff performance, to some degree, on their level of participation? You can measure the number of hits against the site to see who is using it, how frequently they use it and who is not using it. This will give you some metrics about how well the rest of the organization will adopt the new system. It will tell you whether certain types of people prefer this approach and whether other types disapprove.

Watch and learn from the sidelines. Do users still use their conventional methods of communication even though they tell you your system is great? What are they saying in the coffee room (if anything)?

As I said, the technology can be easy or complex. The pilot program gives you a measurement of potential effectiveness before investing heavily in large-scale deployment and training efforts. The more time spent testing and retesting could save your organization much money and time. If you roll out one bad KM system it will be much harder the next time you attempt a repeat because of the lost trust factor.

CHAPTER 10—
Quantifying the results

As I mentioned in other chapters, measuring the effects of knowledge management across the enterprise is still very judgmental and speculative. In order to at least attempt to provide some level of quantifiable impact I would start with the following measures and attempt to build your own along the way. As you find out additional methods I would appreciate greatly if you could send me what you've learned so I can use it. If I put it in a book I'll give you full credits of course.

I've found that you can basically measure results in four different ways; increased levels of performance, increased levels of innovation, level of user participation and profits per professional.

Measuring Performance

Measuring increases in performance is typically a nebulous task. Fortunately we can measure performance with a knowledge management system that specifically targets Explicit knowledge. Remember that the goal of managing Explicit knowledge is to capture the existing process we use on a regular basis, such as a step-by-step process of how to do a specific task. Therefore we can document a specific process and test the time allocated for execution of the process. This allows us to avoid re-inventing the wheel every time someone sits down to perform the same task and sets the metrics by which we can assess the performance of specific individuals assigned to those tasks. This way we have some clear performance measures that can be used to test our staff. Clearly documented processes also can significantly reduce training times.

Measuring Innovation

Measuring for increases in innovation is the measurement of Tacit knowledge exchange, which is difficult but not impossible. We can look for signs of innovative gains in the quality of information entered into programs such as the HELP program we discussed in Chapter 6, the knowledge entered into the project framework and the discussion threads we capture in products such as ListServ. The best way to get a picture of innovation gains is to closely monitor the content of these systems so we can see the types of actions and the evolving thought processes of our people given the quantity and quality of information that is made available to them.

Measuring User Participation

We can also measure the level of user participation in all of our knowledge management systems to see who provides regular input and who capitalizes on the knowledge base asset most frequently. This works for both Tacit and Explicit knowledge. This is the real test of the knowledge management systems we create. The more people utilize data, information and knowledge exchange the more likely they are going to provide the organization more accurate and innovative input. We can use technology to capture these usage statistics making the knowledge manager's job much easier when it comes time to account for the money invested in KM systems. If we can clearly demonstrate a pattern of increased usage then we can assess that the systems are growing as a valuable information resource.

Measuring Profits per Professional

One financial vehicle we can use to measure the effectiveness of a KMS is to track the profitability per professional over time.

A professional is someone directly related to providing the products or services to your clients. This does not include accountants (unless you're an accounting firm), auditors, secretaries or receptionists. These individuals are usually focused on the building of internal structure as opposed to external interface with clients. This also excludes Board Members and typically the senior officers unless they are engaged directly in client interface.

You can use a formula as follows:

Result = (Profit/Revenue) * (Revenue/Total Employees) * (Total Employees/Professionals)

This should provide you with a chart similar to the following:

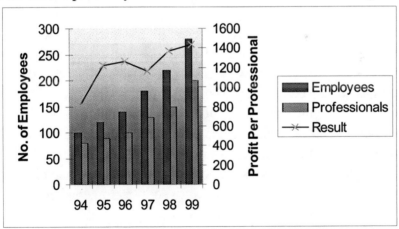

The "result" is the profitability per professional and gives us a key indicator whether we are getting better or poorer results from our professionals over time. If you launch a KMS initiative then you can test over a given period of time. If profitability goes up in a disproportional amount the result may be attributable to either the new KMS and/or the

Hawthorn effect. Of course there are more factors than just a KMS that could affect profitability, so you'll need to factor those into the picture. You should also likely remove the outermost professionals from the salary bell-curve, as they tend to displace the numbers.

One problem with the Profit per Professional is that private companies can "play" with the profitability. Therefore, you need to take into account the effects of accounting for profitability when you decide to use these numbers.

You can also use the proportionality of professionals to other staff as a ratio. The higher the ratio in favor of professionals then the assumption is, the better the organization is managed. You can use your new KMS to track and report this type of information to management as part of the KMS initiative.

If we build a robust knowledge management infrastructure as well as develop the programs necessary to advertise and encourage participation we should see subtle increases in several aspects of our daily lives, such as decreased staff turnover, better staff cooperation, increased levels of staff interaction, increases in available time for process oriented staff as well as a decrease in redundant questions. The effects can be minor or obvious, provided you are looking for them. It is a good idea to assess the state of communication and interaction prior to deployment and retest every so often to get a better feeling of the effects of your KM system.

CHAPTER 11—
Sample Policy

Throughout your organization you will need to create policies to describe and enforce practices in a variety of areas. I'm including a sample policy so you have a frame of reference to build from.

Agency Security Policy

Purpose

The purpose of this Policy is to ensure the security of administrative information that is processed, stored, maintained, or transmitted on computing systems and networks centrally managed by the Agency (*Data*), and to protect the confidentiality of that *Data*. This Policy is designed to protect *Data* from unauthorized change, destruction, or disclosure, whether intentional or accidental.

Scope

Words in bold italics have specific meanings within this document, as described in the Definitions section, below, and determine the scope of the Policy's applicability. This Policy applies to any Agency employees (permanent or temporary) or Agency Contractors who have access to *Data* (*Staff*). It regulates the use of the *Systems,* and applies to all computer programs used to access *Data,* as well as the computers and terminals that run those programs including workstations to which the *Data* has been downloaded.

Community
Intended Audience
The intended audience for the document is all Agency employees.

Beneficiaries
The beneficiaries of this document are the IT staff of Agency.

Document Owner
The owner of this document is Dr. Randy Frid.

Policy
It is the responsibility of *Staff* to protect *Data* from unauthorized change, destruction or disclosure according to Agency, State, Federal or local guidelines, as well as any other regulations or laws which may apply. This Policy governs all Agency maintained central administrative systems that provide access to *Data* (*Systems*) and defines the responsibilities of *Staff* who maintain or use those *Systems*. It should be noted that, in general, Agency is the *Data Owner;* Agency IT Staff is also the *Custodian of the Data.* Agency has total authority to grant or revoke access to *Data* or *Systems* which use *Data.* * It is Agency's responsibility to implement specific procedures which enforce access authority and establish guidelines and standards for *Systems* and *Data* security under this Policy. It is also the Agency's responsibility to establish and promulgate procedures for the dissemination of this Policy. Each individual is responsible for carrying out his or her responsibilities under this Policy.

Violation
Violations of this Policy include, but are not limited to: accessing *Data* or *Systems* which the individual has no legitimate access to; enabling unauthorized individuals to access the *Data*; disclosing *Data* in a way which violates applicable policy, procedure or other relevant

regulations or laws; or inappropriately modifying or destroying *Data*. Violations may result in access revocation, corrective action up to and including dismissal, and/or civil or criminal prosecution under applicable law. Recourse under this Policy is available under the appropriate section of the employee's personnel Policy or contract, or by pursuing applicable legal procedure.

Definitions

Custodian of the Data: the entity or office that is delegated by the *Data Owner* the responsibility of performing management functions for the *Data*.

Data: administrative information which is processed, stored, maintained, or transmitted on computing systems and networks centrally managed by Agency.

Data Owner: the entity or office that is authorized to collect and manage the *Data* as official record.

Staff: any Agency employee (permanent or temporary) or Agency Contractors who have access to *Data*.

Systems: all Agency maintained central administrative systems that provide access to *Data*.

Franchise Site: an external entity that participates in the Agency infrastructure security and administrative boundaries, typically under a service level agreement (SLA).

Standards for Computer Accounts on Agency Systems

Appropriate system-specific standards should be created locally for each *System* (as defined above). There are at least four areas in which

System standards must be defined: authorization to access, termination of computer access, safeguarding accounts and passwords, and user-identification and password standards. Standards in other areas may be added as appropriate for the individual *Systems*.

Following below, are the Agency Standards for Computer Accounts:

Authorization to Access

Only those users who have valid business reasons (as determined by the *Data Owner*) for accessing computers, *Systems,* or *Data* will be granted access. Access privileges are determined by a person's job duties. Access is granted by means of a computer account which has an associated user-id.**

Access is to be used only for the specific business purposes required to process the *Data.*

Termination of Computer Access

When a user no longer works for the Agency or assumes different job duties within the Agency, it is the responsibility of their manager or supervisor to request that their user-id be deleted, at the latest, by the date of termination or transfer. If a transferred employee needs access in a new job, a new user-id must be obtained. User-ids will be terminated if they are not used for one fiscal year.

Access to computer accounts may be suspended at any time if security violations or misuse are suspected. A user-id will be suspended when an incorrect password is entered three consecutive times.

------

* The *Data Owner* may delegate to the *Custodian* the authority to grant access to the *Data* as required for management functions.

Safeguarding Accounts and Passwords

Access to computer accounts must be protected, at minimum, by a user-identification (user-id) and password. It is the responsibility of the user to safeguard his/her user-id and password. A user-id is not to be shared; the password is not to be divulged to others.

User-Identification and Password Standards

A user-id and password must be required to access any system.

A user-id must be at least six characters long.

Passwords must be at least nine characters long.

Passwords must contain at least three non-standard characters (not including A-Z, 0-9)

Passwords must be changed at least once every 90 days.

Data Security Policy

Application Security Administrator

Each application system shall have an Application Security Administrator designated by the *Data Owner.* This individual is responsible for authorizing access privileges to the application, for ensuring that employees who receive user-ids have proper authorization, and for monitoring *Data* access violations. All such authorizations and approvals must be in writing.

System Security Administrator

Each computer system shall have a designated System Security Administrator. This individual is responsible for creating user-ids with the associated access privileges granted by the appropriate Application Security Administrator, for maintaining an appropriate level of overall system security, and for monitoring the system for security violations. This individual shall also maintain records for all accounts including appropriate signatures and associated access privileges granted. Such records shall be maintained for two years after account termination.

Individual Responsibilities

Individual employees are responsible for maintaining the security and confidentiality of *Data* in their possession, such as hardcopy reports or *Data* downloaded to their workstations. Individuals must report to the appropriate security administrator any known breach of application or system security. Individuals who have constructive suggestions to improve security are encouraged to propose them.

Training and Testing

Application system developers and installers shall provide user training on security issues when new *Systems* are installed.

Copies of production *Data* should not be used for purposes that may compromise the confidentiality of individuals or organizations.

Separation of Responsibilities

There shall be a distinct separation of job duties and responsibilities such that no one person has the authority and the ability to circumvent the normal checks and balances of the *Systems*. For example, except for an organization that has a sole programmer, no single individual should hold the responsibilities as an Application Programmer and Production Control personnel; or Application Programmer and Database Administrator; or Production Control personnel and Database Administrator. For applications that contain mission-critical, financial or confidential data, maintenance responsibility for the data-

---

** The "computer account" should not be confused with a "citizen account".

base and system software shall reside in a separate organizational unit than responsibility for the application code. The approval of access privileges to an application shall be in a separate unit from that of the implementer of the access privileges.

Data Disposition

All *Data* shall be properly disposed of when it has exceeded its required retention period, or it is no longer needed for the operation of the Agency. This includes output such as paper listings, CDs, magnetic tapes, microfiche, etc.

Procedure for Dissemination of Security Policy
Policy Availability

This Policy and its associated Guidelines and Standards shall be readily available to all affected *Staff* in departments that have business reasons for accessing the *Data*. Availability may be either in paper or electronic form, and should include references to other relevant policies.

Distribution to New Users

As part of the authorization and approval of new accounts on *Systems* all *Staff* applicants will be given a copy of this Policy and its associated Guidelines and Standards. All *Staff* applicants will be required to sign a statement that they have read the Policy and that they agree to comply with its provisions.

Distribution to Current Users

Each System Security Administrator shall distribute to departments, lists of *Staff* who are currently authorized users of their *Systems*. Agency departmental managers and supervisors must obtain a signed agreement from current *Staff* who have accounts accessing *Data,* stating that they have read this Policy and that they agree to comply with its provisions. Failure to sign will result in the suspension of their user-id.

Methodology

NT Domain structure

The Exchange implementation calls for a single Windows NT domain for all Exchange servers and Domain Controllers within Agency. All Exchange servers will be setup as Stand-alone servers.

Recommendation

NT Domain security

Within the Agency domain, the following accounts are deemed "system accounts" and are explained below.

Accounts in Agency domain	Comments
Administrative Account	*"Administrator"* is to be renamed
Override Accounts	One for entire organization
Exchange Accounts	One for entire organization
SQL Accounts	One for entire organization
MTS Accounts	One for entire organization
SMS Accounts	One for entire organization
Tape Back-up Accounts	One for entire organization
Anti-Virus Accounts	One for entire organization

Administrator Account

The administrator account in Agency domain will be renamed for security reasons, and not be used. The password will be at least 9 characters long, with the combination of alpha and numeric characters. The password should be changed quarterly.

Override Account

The administrator back-up account in Agency domain will be used in the event the primary administrator account is corrupted. The password will be at least 9 characters long, with the combination of alpha and numeric characters. The password should be changed quarterly.

Additional System Accounts

Additional system accounts will be required for individual major services such as e-mail servers, database servers, web servers, management servers, tape back-up services and anti-virus protection. Additional system accounts may be added in the future at the discretion of the Agency information services manager. Serious consideration should be given to each current and additional service account, as there are long-term ramifications for such actions. Many services on many servers may all use a particular account whose password is known to specific Agency IT employees and contractors. Should one of these individuals leave the Agency then policy should dictate the changing of the system account passwords that were associated and known to the departing employee or contractor. This would require a detailed process to ensure that all applications and servers are updated simultaneously across the organization and within each related service running on each server.

Therefore, system accounts will be created based on type of service using the account and knowledge of the system account password must be carefully guarded with a specific Agency IT employee being assigned ownership of each password, preferably one password per person. A copy of each system account password will be sealed and locked in a secure environment that permits only the IT Section Head access should something happen to the individual with privileged access to the password.

The Agency will **NEVER** create a generic service account, as it will become common to use this account in the event no specialized system account exists. It will not take long before Agency IT staff loses track of the number of applications and services using this generic account that will cause significant problems when the need to change the password arises.

Password administration

The service account password will be changed after installation of all sites. Because of the steps needed for service account password change (Exchange admin, NT services, and connector override), "force password change" is not recommended for the service account. Instead, service account password changes will be performed on a scheduled basis, and based upon well-documented procedure.

Audit

By default, Exchange server system logs and application logs are visible to anyone that has been authenticated on the server. However, local administrator rights are required for security logs. The security log rights are limited to selected local site administrators to monitor possible security violation.

Backup ID security

ArcServe needs to have the backup id within the domain in order to accommodate smooth backup and restore operations. These accounts will have the permissions that meet their specific requirement.

Summary of NT security recommendations:

Rights and permission	Agency domain accounts		
	Administrator	Service account	Override account
Password composition	1 Capital 1 numeric 1 punctuation 6 other characters	> 8 characters, consist of both alpha and numeric	> 8 characters, consist of both alpha and numeric
Periodic change password	Quarterly	Annually	Quarterly
Logon locally	Yes	No	No
Event: System	Yes	No	Yes
Event: Application	Yes	No	Yes
Event: Security	Yes	No	No

Exchange Security

The Agency Information Systems staff for Exchange will consist of only two individuals. Both will be granted full administrative rights into the Exchange organization but only one will hold the permissions to the Exchange System Account password. They will be able perform any administrative task required within the organization. However, for the purpose of completeness and future planning, the following information is provided to allow Agency to easily extend the IT staff and still maintain a secure Exchange network.

Tape Backup Account Security

Tape Backup account permissions for Exchange is unique for different software vendors. In general, at least *"permission admin"* rights are required for backup to work. Agency needs to consult their specific backup software manual.

Service Account Security

All service accounts for core service sites will reside in AGENCY resource domain. This configuration will facilitate more reliable site connection, and easier management.

No logon local rights

No service accounts will have "logon locally rights", as to prevent unauthorized logon into AGENCY domain.

Printed in the United States
98626LV00005B/439/A